Cover Art: Lester E. Potts, Jr.
(painted during mid-stage Alzheimer's disease)
To view more of Lester's art, visit
www.lestersleqacy.com.

Author Photo: Maxine Picard
(Taken at the David W. Streets Gallery, Beverly Hills, CA)

A POCKET GUIDE
FOR THE
ALZHEIMER'S CAREGIVER

This book is dedicated to our family members with Alzheimer's disease and other forms of dementia, and their caregivers:

Lucille and George Chapman
Hazel Enloe
Jo Chapman Gibson
Lola Brandon Juergens
Kate Enloe Monk
Ernestine Smiley Oaks
Ethelda (Oaks) and Lester Potts
Margaret Enloe Woodward
Mary (Chapman) and George Woodward

This book is meant to be a helpful guide to caregivers of those with Alzheimer's disease. It is not meant to be an exhaustive reference, nor is it a substitute for the evaluation or care of a qualified healthcare practitioner. Recommendations given may work with some people, but not with others. The behavior of those with Alzheimer's disease and other cognitive disabilities can be unpredictable. If the person for whom you are caring needs medical attention, or if you are unable to care for him or her alone, you should consult a qualified healthcare practitioner.

ACKNOWLEDGEMENTS

First and foremost, this book would not be possible if not for the example of selfless caregiving we have watched in our own family members, and the difficulties we saw in our loved ones with Alzheimer's disease and other forms of dementia. Without their example and others like theirs, "A Pocket Guide for the Alzheimer's Caregiver" would never have been written.

Additionally, we are deeply indebted to Dr. Robert C. Griggs for writing the Foreword, and to the American Academy of Neurology, whose Palatucci Advocacy Leadership Forum trained Daniel for effective Alzheimer's advocacy.

Our thanks to friends and family members who helped edit the book for content and grammar errors: Ann Killingsworth Jones, Ethelda Oaks Potts, and Mary Chapman Woodward. If the book is error-free, please give them the credit. If you find errors, we claim them as our own! We express our gratitude to Professor Gorazd Bernard Stokin, M.D., who proofread, gave suggestions and has offered to translate our book into various European languages.

Vicki Van Valkenburgh provided invaluable expertise in navigating the waters of the publishing and social media world. Also, we are grateful to Maxine Picard for our author photograph, which was taken at a showing of Daniel's father's art at the David W. Streets Gallery in Beverly Hills, California.

FOREWORD

Each of us depends upon caregivers after we are born. Most of us will depend upon caregivers again before we die. And most of us will be faced with the challenge of being a caregiver for someone else. But the burdens of being a caregiver and the skills needed to do it well --- and enjoy caregiving --- are unfamiliar territory for everyone. Only recently have we recognized that quantitating caregiver burden and reducing it by appropriate treatment has an importance equal to that of treating a patient.

Alzheimer's disease places tremendous responsibilities and burdens upon families. The burdens of caring for 5 million Americans with Alzheimer's disease represent a challenge of almost unimaginable magnitude.

In this book two healthcare professionals team up to provide an action-oriented, proactive approach to caring for patients --- usually a loved one --- with Alzheimer's disease. The book is the place for the frightened to turn to for initial information and perspective on Alzheimer's disease --- and then to return to for practical advice as problems arise. Most importantly, however, it dispels the sense of hopelessness families may feel by providing steps to maximize the enjoyment of life for the patient with Alzheimer's disease.

Neurologist Dr. Daniel Potts ("Danny" to nearly everyone) speaks from immense personal experience, both as a son whose father developed Alzheimer's disease, and then, as an advocate for steps to improve the enjoyment of life by patients with Alzheimer's disease. These efforts were so successful that he was named Advocate of the Year by the American Academy of Neurology in 2008. Danny's father, never an artist, developed an interest in painting, and his artwork became a source of joy to him and of wonder to his family and friends. It became his way of expressing his unique personality even as the illness progressed. Danny's success has made him a mentor for other neurologists who want to advocate for solutions to helping patients and families with neurological disease.

Danny Potts brings his neurological skills and Ellen Potts her administrative and managerial expertise to provide clear, concise and practical perspective and advice on the care of Alzheimer's disease. This is a book that anyone who has the opportunity to help care for and improve the life of patients with Alzheimer's disease will want to read and return to: Family members, nurses, and other health care professionals. Judging from my own interest in the book, it also gives important perspective to physicians and physicians-in-training.

Robert C. Griggs, M.D., FAAN

Professor of Neurology, Medicine, Pediatrics,
    Pathology & Laboratory Medicine and Center
    for Human Experimental Therapeutics
President (2009 - 2011), American Academy of
    Neurology
Editor-in-Chief (1997 - 2007), *Neurology*

INTRODUCTION

"Courage doesn't always roar. Sometimes courage is the quiet voice at the end of the day saying, 'I will try again tomorrow.'" --- Mary Anne Radmacher

This should be the mantra of the Alzheimer's caregiver. They have one of the most difficult jobs imaginable, and because of their love, dedication, and courage, give their best day after day.

We two authors have had 8 relatives with Alzheimer's disease or other forms of dementia for whom our immediate families provided care. These loved ones lived in or received daycare from 15 different facilities. In our experience with family caregivers, employed caregivers, and in Daniel's medical practice, we have found so many struggling to give the best possible care without adequate tools and training resources. In response, we formed Dementia Dynamics to help educate caregivers, whether they are employed or taking care of loved ones. This book was born of these experiences, from our research, from Daniel's background in neurology and from our passion to help those with Alzheimer's disease and their caregivers.

It is our desire to provide very practical, quickly-accessed information to Alzheimer's caregivers. These techniques often work with those suffering from other forms of dementia, but we will primarily address Alzheimer's disease. The book is divided into two sections --- the first with discussions of common issues and problems, and the second with an alphabetical quick reference of problems and listed responses. We give many examples, but the names of non-family members have been changed to protect privacy.

We hope you find this book helpful. You and your fellow caregivers remain in our thoughts and prayers. We must all encourage one another in this Herculean task.

Daniel C. Potts, MD
Ellen Woodward Potts

TABLE OF CONTENTS

PART I: COMMON ISSUES

PART II: QUICK REFERENCE

PART I

COMMON ISSUES

Chapter 1

ALZHEIMER'S DISEASE: THE BASICS

What is Alzheimer's disease?

Alzheimer's disease is a progressive, incurable disorder of the brain, which keeps a person from storing memories properly. As time goes on, it affects a person's brain function in other ways and takes away the ability to perform normal daily living tasks. Alzheimer's disease is the most common cause of **dementia,** a group of conditions which impair a person's thinking abilities to the point where they can no longer function completely independently. Alzheimer's disease is but one of many causes of dementia, including stroke and vascular disease, fronto-temporal dementia, dementia with Lewy Bodies, alcoholic dementia, Parkinson's disease, normal pressure hydrocephalus, and others. Some causes of dementia are treatable, like vitamin B 12 deficiency. The symptoms of Alzheimer's disease are treatable to some degree, but the disease is not curable at this point.

In the United states currently there are approximately 5.4 million individuals with Alzheimer' disease, and it is the sixth leading cause of death. The number of cases is expected to rise to 11 to 16 million by 2050, and it is estimated that 10 million "baby-boomers" will get the disease. Every 70 seconds someone in the U.S. develops

Alzheimer's disease. Ten percent of 65 year-olds and nearly 50% of 85 year-olds have the disease. There are almost 15 million Alzheimer's and dementia caregivers in the U.S., and the total cost of the illness to our healthcare system is $183 billion annually.[1]

Alzheimer's disease is typically a disease of older people, though in rare cases it affects younger adults. Risk factors for the disease include old age, positive family history of the illness, female sex, prior history of head injury, prior history of depression, heart and vascular disease, high blood pressure, diabetes, high cholesterol, Latin American or African American heritage, Down's Syndrome, and low educational level. Alzheimer's disease is not strongly inherited in general, though having a close relative who gets Alzheimer's at a younger age increases your risk. A growing body of research shows evidence that things that are bad for your heart are also bad for your brain (like hypertension, diabetes, sleep apnea and high cholesterol). By the same token, things that are good for your heart are also good for your brain, like exercise and the Mediterranean-style diet (the combination of which may lower one's risk of dementia by 50%). For more information on the Mediterranean diet, go to http://www.mayoclinic.com/health/mediterranean-diet/CL00011

Alzheimer's disease is thought to be caused by malfunctioning proteins in the brain. Amyloid, a protein which we all have in our brains, "clumps" together in an abnormal way after it is sliced up by

---

1 Alzheimer's Association, http://www.alz.org/alzheimers_disease_facts_and_figures.asp

brain enzymes in the person with Alzheimer's. These "clumps" of amyloid are believed damage brain cells, and cause the immune system to come in and "clean up the mess." The cleaning process damages other nerve cells, and results in one of the main features of the disease, **senile plaques**. Another protein, Tau, becomes malformed and interferes with the function of the cells, resulting in another main feature of the disease, **neurofibrillary tangles**. The combined effect of these and other processes disrupt brain connections and cause the death of brain cells. The brain progressively loses function and shrinks as tissue dies. This is most noted in the region of the brain responsible for short-term memory (the hippocampus). There is atrophy (shrinkage) in other brain regions as well.

This loss of brain cells and their connections and function results in **10 warning signs of the illness:**

1. Short-term memory loss that disrupts daily life
2. Difficulties in planning or solving problems
3. Difficulty completing familiar tasks
4. Confusion with time or place
5. Trouble understanding what one sees
6. New problems with words in speaking or writing
7. Misplacing things and losing the ability to retrace steps
8. Decreased or poor judgment
9. Withdrawal from work or social activities

10. Changes in mood and personality[2]

And the **4 "A's" of Alzheimer's disease:**

1. Amnesia - short term memory loss
2. Aphasia - language disturbance
3. Apraxia - the inability to perform learned tasks
4. Agnosia - inability to recognize familiar people or objects[3]

The hallmark of Alzheimer's disease is the **gradual progression** of short-term memory loss and other brain deficits. The problems are subtle at first, and may not significantly interfere with daily living. This stage is known as **Mild Cognitive Impairment (MCI)**. MCI progresses to dementia at a rate of about 10% per year. People with MCI should be followed closely for worsening. No medication has been clearly shown to delay the progression of MCI to Alzheimer's disease, though the behavioral interventions (primarily exercise, the Mediterranean diet, cognitive stimulation and the maintenance of social interaction) should be emphasized at this stage.

In addition to the above, people with Alzheimer's disease may display other symptoms as well. Uncharacteristic behaviors or depression are often initial features. Alzheimer's sufferers often are paranoid ("somebody is stealing my money," "you and your brother just want to put me away," "my husband is having an affair," etc.). Paranoia can be

---

[2] Alzheimer's Association, http://www.alz.org/alzheimers_disease_10_signs_of_alzheimers.asp

[3] http://www.alzbrain.org/pdf/handouts/2003.%20DEMENTIA.pdf

especially trying for the caregiver, who is often the person accused.

Individuals may become lost in familiar territory, forget how to perform common household tasks, and misplace items. Some with the disease become uncharacteristically anxious or belligerent, and some become docile. People with Alzheimer's disease have "good days and bad days," and the function, mood and mental abilities of the person greatly depend on sleep, diet, stress level, and other things in the person's daily life.

As the disease progresses, your loved one will be more and more dependent on you and other caregivers to remain functional. She will have increasing difficulties with activities of daily living, such as feeding herself, dressing, toileting, and bathing. Expect her to become frustrated at her loss of physical and mental capabilities. As the disease progresses, your loved one may be unable to express basic needs and desires, such as the urge to go to the bathroom, to eat, to scratch an itch, to adjust from a painful position, etc. This may cause her to become agitated, and it will be difficult for you as the caregiver to know what to do to help. Though you should enable her to have as much independence as possible, safety is an ever-present concern. Err on the side of safety rather than independence. The time will come when you will need help. **Do not wait until your physical or mental health is in jeopardy to seek it!** Pursue dementia daycare or dementia residential care facilities earlier rather than later. These entities often have structured, stimulating environments that may be better for the person than staying at home. Trained sitters also are a possibility. We cover these options later in this book.

The typical life expectancy after one has been diagnosed with Alzheimer's disease is 7 to 10 years. If a person makes it to end-stage disease, he is typically bed-bound, cannot speak, is incontinent, and cannot carry out any tasks for himself. Rarely can a person be cared for at home in such a state; usually by this time the individual has been placed in either a specialty care locked dementia unit in an assisted living facility, or a nursing home. Death in Alzheimer's disease is usually from a secondary condition like aspiration pneumonia or a severe urinary tract infection. Hospice is a very valuable option for care of a person with late stage Alzheimer's. In our experience with our own loved ones, this is the most humane and compassionate option available, and we strongly support its use.

The diagnosis of Alzheimer's disease is typically made on clinical grounds by examining the person, performing short tests of memory and cognitive abilities, and imaging the brain with an MRI (or sometimes a CT). Neuro-psychologic testing may be performed in unusual cases or if depression is thought to be present (which can masquerade as dementia). Also, a doctor will order blood work to rule out treatable conditions like B 12 deficiency or thyroid or kidney disease. PET scanning (a specialized radiology procedure which tests the function of the brain) is rarely necessary, and we do not advocate the use of spinal taps or genetic testing to make the diagnosis at this point, though these may be used to diagnose the illness before it is causing symptoms when a cure or effective preventions become available (see below).

If no reversible cause of dementia is found, the person is often started on a medication to improve cognitive function or slow down its decline. The medications typically used are donepezil (Aricept), rivastigmine (Exelon), galantamine (Razadyne) or memantine (Namenda). The choice of medication depends on several factors. Follow the physician's recommendations regarding medication choice. In the course of the illness, the person's behavior may become difficult to manage, requiring medical treatment. Certain antidepressants, antipsychotics, and mood stabilizing medications (such as valproic acid, or Depakote) may be prescribed. These may be very effective, but also have side effects. Be sure and request counseling on side effects with any new medication prescribed. Many other potential treatments are on the way, including medications that will attack the very pathologic processes that cause the illness. However, most agree that a cure is not on the immediate horizon. For this reason, **care makes all the difference** (to borrow a slogan from an excellent organization, The Alzheimer's Foundation of America).

The Stages of Alzheimer's Disease

Though Alzheimer's disease usually progresses persistently and gradually, some physicians divide the disease into stages to help caregivers know what to expect. Up to 7 stages are discussed, but we prefer to think of 3: mild, moderate and severe (or as some refer to them, early, middle and late).

In the **Mild / Early Alzheimer's stage**, people may experience the following:

- ***Memory loss for recent events:*** Individuals may have an especially hard time remembering newly learned information and repeatedly ask the same question.
- ***Difficulty with problem solving, complex tasks and sound judgments:*** Planning a family event or balancing a checkbook may become overwhelming. Many people experience lapses in judgment, such as when making financial decisions.
- ***Changes in personality:*** People may become subdued or withdrawn (especially in socially challenging situations) or show uncharacteristic irritability or anger. Decreased attention span and reduced motivation to complete tasks also are common.
- ***Difficulty organizing and expressing thoughts:*** Finding the right words to describe objects or clearly express ideas becomes increasingly challenging.
- ***Getting lost or misplacing belongings:*** Individuals have increasing trouble finding their way around, even in familiar places. It's also common to lose or misplace things, including valuable items.

In the **Moderate / Middle Alzheimer's stage,** people may experience the following:

- ***Increasingly poor judgment and deepening confusion:*** Individuals lose track of where they are, the day of the week or the season. They often lose the ability to recognize their own belongings and may inadvertently take things that don't belong to them. Also, they may confuse family members or close friends with one another, or mistake strangers for family. They often wander, possibly in search of surroundings that feel more familiar and "right." These difficulties make it unsafe to leave those in the moderate Alzheimer's stage by themselves.

- ***Greater memory loss***: People may forget details of their personal history, such as their address or phone number, or where they attended school. They repeat favorite stories or make up stories to fill gaps in memory.
- ***Increased need for help with some daily activities***: Assistance may be required with choosing proper clothing and with bathing, grooming, using the bathroom and other self-care tasks. Some individuals occasionally lose control of their urine or bowel movements.
- ***Significant changes in personality and behavior***: It is not unusual for people with moderate Alzheimer's to develop unfounded suspicions — for example, to become convinced that friends, family or professional caregivers are stealing from them, or that a spouse is having an affair. Others may see or hear things that aren't really there. Individuals often grow restless or agitated, especially late in the day ("sundowning"). People may have outbursts of accusing, threatening or cursing. Others may bite, kick, scream or attempt inappropriate sexual activity.

In the **Severe / Late Alzheimer's stage**, people may experience

- ***Loss of the ability to communicate coherently***: An individual can no longer converse or speak coherently, although he or she may occasionally say words or phrases.

- ***Increased daily assistance with personal care***: This includes total assistance with eating, dressing, using the bathroom and all other daily self-care tasks.
- ***Decline in physical abilities***: A person may become unable to walk without assistance, then unable to sit or hold up his or her head without support. Muscles may become rigid and reflexes abnormal. Eventually, a person loses the ability to swallow and to control bladder and bowel functions.

Recently, three international workgroups convened by the Alzheimer's Association and the National Institute on Aging (NIA) issued the first new criteria and guidelines to diagnose Alzheimer's disease in 27 years. Though largely confined to the research community at this point, these criteria will be more widely utilized as advances in diagnostic technologies become available in community settings. The articles — collectively, the National Institute on Aging/Alzheimer's Association Diagnostic Guidelines for Alzheimer's Disease — expand the definition of Alzheimer's to include: (1) **pre-symptomatic** and (2) **mildly symptomatic but pre-dementia**, along with (3) **dementia caused by Alzheimer's**. This reflects current thinking that Alzheimer's begins creating distinct and measurable changes in the brains of affected people years, perhaps decades, before memory and thinking symptoms are noticeable. In fact, certain biological changes (biomarkers) that can be measured by MRI and PET scanning have been identified, and may predict who will get the disease decades before any symptoms occur. These are exciting developments, and offer hope for early diagnosis that most certainly will be paired with effective medical treatments in the coming years.

"We have a diagnosis. Now what?"

The diagnosis of Alzheimer's disease, much like the diagnosis of cancer, can be devastating. Healthcare providers often have differing opinions on whether a person afflicted with the disease should be told they have Alzheimer's. We err on the side of not using the term Alzheimer's when discussing the condition with the patient, but using "dementia" instead, thinking such a term may lessen a sense of hopelessness or depressed feelings. The family and caregivers, however, are always told the diagnosis. We fully acknowledge that not every healthcare provider has this approach. We do share the term "Alzheimer's" with quite a few patients based on our assessment of each case. That being said, there is some recent evidence that seems to suggest telling people they have Alzheimer's disease may not significantly increase their likelihood of depression. One critical point should be made here: the person **must** be told he has a condition that is affecting his brain function. Otherwise, he will wonder why he is being taken to the doctor, placed on medication, assisted with daily activities, etc.

As soon as possible after you are aware of the diagnosis, we recommend you begin taking steps to prepare for the road ahead. Caring for a person with Alzheimer's disease is very costly, in both financial and human terms. Long-term care insurance is a good idea, but once a person is diagnosed with Alzheimer's disease, it is difficult or impossible to find a company which will issue a policy. Even this option will not begin to fully cover the cost of care. Plan now for the likelihood that your loved one will need dementia assisted living or nursing home care. In addition, while your loved one is still able to express his wishes, estate planning, wills, living wills, and other decisions regarding healthcare and end of life should be made and documented, if he has not already done so. It is very important that your loved one be given the opportunity to provide direction in his care. This is still possible for most people in the early stages of the disease. Furthermore, such action will relieve some of your burden as a caregiver when tough decisions arise along the way.

We strongly recommend that you seek the assistance of an eldercare attorney soon after the diagnosis. These individuals have the expertise to guide you down the very confusing road of long-term care planning. Medicaid, the primary state-run funding program for long-term care, has an extremely complicated and ever-changing set of eligibility requirements and rules which only an experienced eldercare attorney practicing in the state where the person with Alzheimer's lives (VERY important) is qualified to interpret. If you don't know where to find an eldercare attorney, check with your state's nearest school of law, as many times they have these departments on campus. Otherwise, check with the state bar association for a list of qualified eldercare attorneys.

It is also advisable to sit down and put together a care plan for your loved one which incorporates "off" time for you. This is a very important element, as you will not be able to make it in this "marathon" without rest and tending to your own needs. We suggest finding your nearest Alzheimer's caregiver support group and attending meetings. For some, listening to caregiver stories can be frightening, especially soon after you have begun your role as caregiver. In the long run the shared support and affirmation will be helpful to you and other caregivers.

Driving safety (addressed later in this book) should always be a primary concern. Get into the habit of paying careful attention to your loved one's driving performance, and report to his physician the first signs of difficulty. It can be argued that by the time an individual has gotten a diagnosis of Alzheimer's disease, he should no longer drive. In some cases and in early stage disease, driving still can occur safely, but we recommend leaning toward safety and transitioning your loved one from the driver's side to the passenger's side.

Likewise, begin to carefully observe your loved one's ability to handle financial responsibilities. As will be stated elsewhere in the book, it is important to give your loved one as much independence as possible. However, too much independence in the face of inability may be harmful. If your husband begins to make mistakes with the checkbook and you continue to allow him to pay bills, he may be very embarrassed when made aware of mistakes he has made. He may become paranoid and defensive about it. Other financial precautions also should be taken. Place your loved one on the national "do not call" list for all solicitations. One family member with Alzheimer's disease often received cold calls from stock brokers and would place large orders, completely forgetting he had done so. You may imagine the chaos it caused when the bills arrived.

Just as with financial responsibilities, you need to monitor your loved one carefully to determine when it is appropriate to take away duties or restrict tasks. For instance, Ellen's grandfather always had repaired their cars, lawnmowers, and other things around the house. One day, her grandmother came into the garage to find he had taken most of the engine parts out of the car, but could not put them back together. It is a difficult balancing act to decide when it is appropriate to restrict your loved one. Sometimes, you will be too cautious. Other times, you will wait too long. Unfortunately, there is no formula by which you can calculate when the time is right, but we encourage you to err on the side of caution.

Make sure the issue of taking medication correctly is also taken care of early on. People with Alzheimer's typically are on several medications, and the scheduling of doses may be difficult. We recommend the use of a pill box that is divided by date and dosing time, and that this be checked every day by the caregiver, even if you do not live in the same physical location as your loved one. Calendars and reminders of upcoming activities should be employed early on as well, so that your loved can develop habits of checking these memory aids. Routine, routine, **ROUTINE** is extremely important and should be developed early. Important phone numbers and addresses should be placed in easy-to-access locations, and home modifications should occur at this time (see later sections of this book). It would be a good idea to go ahead and investigate the availability of trained dementia sitters in your community for the time when they may be needed. You should also inform your family and friends about the steps you are taking, so that they may assist you in caring for your loved one, and so that everyone is on the same page. Loan or purchase this book and others on Alzheimer's care to give to family members.

Make every effort to keep scheduled doctor visits, even though it may be increasingly difficult to get your loved one to the office. Prepare an updated list of medications, questions, and concerns to send to the healthcare provider before the visit. This can make care much easier and more effective, and can prevent embarrassing situations from arising in the exam room. Keep an updated list of your loved one's diagnoses and medications on your person for easy access. We cover this subject in greater detail later in the book.

Above all, begin training yourself to **have an attitude of hope** --- to learn to love and appreciate your loved one as he is in his "now". This "now" will be a moving target: he will have good days and bad days, and his overall condition will slowly decline. However, this person is still the one you love, and deep down, he still has gifts and talents and a life story and the ability to give and receive love and affection. Learn to look past loss and see opportunity --- opportunity to experience life with your loved one in a different way. **And you must laugh with them**! Find humor in the mundane, everyday details of life. Sit down and chuckle at your favorite comedy show. Tell jokes. Laugh at the funny things that will arise every day as you care for your loved one. Those of us who have walked the road know that this is an absolute necessity! Although it may sound almost ridiculous to you in your current state, these ideas will surely make more sense as you travel down your path, hand in hand.

At the end of this book you will find a list of caregiver resources you may find helpful along the way. Godspeed in your journey of caregiving --- **a high calling indeed!**

Chapter 2

A WORD ABOUT CAREGIVING

The recurrent theme in our approach to caring for a person with Alzheimer's is the **validation of the human being in such a way as to promote dignity and self worth.** Although Alzheimer's may chip away at memory and other cognitive functions, the core of the human being still remains and must be valued and enriched. Most agree that the emotional self remains, even into the late stage. This means that the person is still able to interpret a smile, a kind voice, a gentle touch, and is able to respond to these and other gestures of caring. Alzheimer's disease does not affect a person's soul. Our goal, along with many others working in this field, is to transform the standard from de-humanizing, task-oriented care to that which has respect for the human core still locked inside the person with Alzheimer's.

All too often, in our experience, the person with Alzheimer's is viewed as one who has "checked out," is no longer consciously present, can no longer interpret or interact with her environment. Family members and employed caregivers alike make comments within hearing distance of the person who is presumed to be beyond understanding. People with Alzheimer's are often ignored as they sit listlessly in wheelchairs in the corner of their rooms. "She's just a vegetable now," we often believe. The person is still a human being who deserves to be treated with kindness, dignity and respect.

While participating in art and music therapy at a local dementia daycare center called Caring Days, Daniel's father, Lester Potts, a rural Alabama saw miller, became an acclaimed watercolor artist after the diagnosis of Alzheimer's disease. Lester had never shown any artistic talent before the diagnosis. Even after he had essentially lost his language function, this man in the late stages of his disease was able to paint abstract representations of his father and childhood home. Lost in his affliction, he was a broken man when he came to Caring Days. However, his caregivers looked past inability and affliction and saw a capable human being still endowed with talents and gifts, though not the ones for which he was known before. They validated Lester in his "here and now" and sought to discover other talents. In this way, Lester's previously unknown artistic abilities were unveiled and appreciated. This discovery and the subsequent fostering improved Lester's quality of life, affirmed him in his current state, validated him as a human being, and bolstered his self worth. As a consequence, Lester's mood, cognition, function and behavior improved, and respite was granted to his wife and primary caregiver. Lester's life was enriched, even in the midst of this tragic illness, because of the quality of the caregiving he received.

This example of validating, person-centered, dignifying care has become our mantra for Alzheimer's caregiving, and is the overriding theme of this handbook. Alzheimer's disease cannot steal the self away from the human being and those who love him.

Chapter 3

GENERAL TIPS FOR INTERACTION

For many years, "Reality Orientation" was the recommended technique for dealing with anyone with Alzheimer's disease. In other words, caregivers were taught they could "reorient" or bring the person with Alzheimer's back to the real world. One of the most extreme examples we have heard using this technique involved a family who was moving their mother into a memory care assisted living unit. The mother was confused and kept asking for her husband. At that point the family would pull out photos of their father's funeral and "reorient" her to the fact that their father was dead. Predictably, the mother dissolved into tears. The family handed the funeral photos to the shocked dementia unit administrator with instructions to show those to their mother anytime she forgot her husband was dead. With Alzheimer's disease, what is kind and what is true are not necessarily the same thing. We advocate for kindness over factual accuracy.

This current school of thought goes by several names --- "Validation therapy" from Naomi Feil, "Habilitation" from Joanne Koenig Coste, "Person-Centered Care" from Tom Kitwood, and several others. The basic premise is this: As time goes on, a person with Alzheimer's is less and less able to connect with the "real world." Caregiver attempts to "reorient" the person will not be successful, because people with Alzheimer's disease lose their ability to remember first the recent past, and then the past in general. They lose their ability to understand reality. Given that, ***love them the way they are***. Affirm them the way they are. Interact with them in their world. Don't try to drag them into yours. Do not focus on the disease, focus on the person with the disease.

What would have been a better response from the family to their mother's belief that her husband was still alive? "Maybe he'll be here before long. Do you remember that time when we all went to the beach?" In this scenario, the family relates a happy memory of their family when their father was still alive. Even if their mother does not remember the particular event, it leaves her with a pleasant feeling about the interaction, rather than a feeling of devastating loss.

Affirm where the person is, who she is, and what she believes. Her fears and beliefs may not be rooted in reality, but they are very real to her. Distract her, affirm her, and make the interaction pleasant. This is most difficult for family caregivers who remember their loved one as a rational, capable human being. Regarding our own loved ones with Alzheimer's, we always thought that if we tried hard enough, corrected them enough, "reoriented" them enough, we could reach that rational person. The truth is that most times this is not possible and constant correction further contributes to the depression that often accompanies dementia.

Our rules of thumb are these:

1. Don't correct! Redirect!

2. Enter the person's world. Don't try to drag him into yours.

3. Always treat the person with kindness, dignity and respect.

As Alzheimer's disease progresses, people lose their ability to do complicated tasks. Their brains can no longer sequence the steps. As the caregiver, you need to break the steps down into manageable-sized tasks. For instance, there are more than 15 steps involved in brushing your teeth. When you say to your loved one, "Brush your teeth," that may be beyond him. His response may very well be, "I don't want to brush my teeth," or "I've already brushed my teeth." In this case, approach it from a different direction. Lead the person into the bathroom, hand him the toothbrush, hand him the toothpaste, and so on until the task is accomplished. The same holds true for bathing, changing clothes, anything that requires multiple steps. Remember that abilities come and go with Alzheimer's disease. A task which is beyond your loved one today may not be tomorrow. Although the general trend is downward over time, there are ups and downs, good days and bad.

Chapter 4

"I WANT TO GO HOME."

This is the ever-present desire of all those with Alzheimer's disease. As everything loses familiarity, they search for that most basic place of safety: Home. The problem is that "home" may not be the place where the person is living now. To Ellen's grandfather who had Alzheimer's disease, the home where he lived from 1960 - 1983 when he died was unfamiliar. He wanted to go back to Limestone, TN, the community in which he lived from age 9 to 24, moving away by 1929. In Limestone not much had changed since his childhood. The WPA had brought electricity and running water in the late 1930's and early 40's, but otherwise, it looked much the same. However, he did not recognize it. "I want to go home. I want to go to Limestone," he would say as the family drove him through this tiny community. To those with Alzheimer's, nothing looks familiar. Nowhere is home. In our opinion this is one of the most devastating consequences of the disease.

This lack of recognition of home can be particularly problematic for the caregiver. If your loved one constantly wants to go home, it increases the likelihood he will wander away. Perhaps he will go to the mailbox, begin the return to the house, not recognize it, and wander off. Please take precautions against wandering (see **WANDERING**) if your loved one with Alzheimer's disease can walk. The risks of tragedy if he wanders away are too great.

To help your loved one find the "familiar," there are several things you can do. One way is through "reminiscence therapy," a technique using old photographs, old stories, favorite music, and / or familiar readings. Most of those with Alzheimer's disease remember things from the distant past, but not the recent past. Go through old photographs of friends and family. Listen to the person's favorite music from his teens and twenties. Sing those songs with him. Watch favorite old movies from the person's teens and twenties. Read familiar books, scripture, and poetry --- anything that helps the person feel safe and the environment seem familiar.

Art therapy often can tease out familiar memories from the person. Daniel's father, Lester Potts, was able to draw or paint things from his distant past, even after he had lost his language function almost entirely. Music therapy is also beneficial. When Lester was admitted to an inpatient hospice unit at the end of his life, he had not spoken in several months. However, even less than 24 hours before his death, we discovered he could still sing the familiar hymns he learned in childhood. It gave him something familiar, and it gave us a way to connect with him.

Whatever helps the person feel safe and loved will help him feel at home.

Chapter 5

FALSE ACCUSATIONS

One of the most common issues caregivers face is repeated false accusations, most commonly that someone (perhaps the caregiver) is stealing from the person with Alzheimer's. The items stolen could be money or anything else, valuable or invaluable. You must realize that the person's belief and her paranoia are very real to her. You cannot convince her otherwise. When accused of stealing or anything else, try not to argue, defend yourself or get upset. It is the disease talking, not the person behind the disease.

Accusations of stealing are common because an inability to find things goes hand in glove with Alzheimer's disease. The person forgets where she put something and cannot find it. Therefore, someone must have stolen it. Is it not always easier to blame someone else than to blame yourself?

If the person lives in a facility, someone very well may have taken whatever she is looking for. Alzheimer's disease facilities are for people with memory issues. All of them have trouble remembering what is theirs and what belongs to someone else. Label everything in permanent marker, and usually it will come back to the rightful owner. Take nothing of real value (jewelry, furs, etc.) to a facility unless you are taking the person on an outing. Then, take those items home with you again. Also, you can replace expensive items with similar ones of lesser value. For instance, replace a diamond ring with a similar cubic zirconium, a fur coat with a fake, or a nice watch with one from the drug store.

How should you deal with accusations of theft? Again, the belief is real to the person, and you will only upset her by arguing. Any action on the caregiver's part must start from that understanding. "Let me help you look for it. Maybe the thief dropped it somewhere around here," is a good response. Begin by looking for the item, but help her get distracted along the way. "Find" something else: an old photo album, a favorite CD, a piece of artwork made by a grandchild --- anything that can take her mind off the "stolen" item.

Another strategy is to tell your loved one anything that will allay her fears about the object. Your mother believes her favorite bracelet has been stolen? "Mama, I took it out to be cleaned. It really was looking tarnished." Your father believes someone has taken his blue sport coat? "Dad, there was a seam that had torn, so I took it home to repair it." Technically, this is telling the person a lie. However, you are lying to allay fears in a fear-filled world, not for malicious intent. In the world of a person with Alzheimer's disease, the world is losing its familiarity. Playing along with what the person is saying and calming those fears, even if it technically means not telling the truth, may be the kindest thing you can do.

Chapter 6

HALLUCINATIONS, ALTERED PERCEPTIONS and FEARS

Those with Alzheimer's disease have perceptions of the world that often bear little or no resemblance to reality.

Reflections: A man looks in the mirror and sees a long-dead relative, a frightening stranger, a friend with whom to have a conversation --- any number of comforting or frightening images. Often these images bear no resemblance to reality. As time goes on, most people with Alzheimer's lose their ability to recognize themselves in the mirror because they remember themselves as being much younger. Windows or any type of reflective surface can cause the same problem. If the person begins seeing frightening images in reflections, take down or cover the mirrors. This is especially important in the bathroom or bedroom where a person may become frightened (even to the point of violence) if he sees a stranger in the mirror while a caregiver is dressing or undressing him.

Television / Movies: Those with Alzheimer's often believe what is happening on the television or on a movie screen is happening in the room with them. Daniel's grandmother believed that Dan Rather came personally to her home every afternoon to tell her the day's news. Before Mr. Rather arrived, she would put on her make-up, fix her hair, and make certain she was dressed well for her guest. This is a humorous and harmless altered perception. However, if she had believed the war was occurring in her living room, or the criminal on a police show was in her house, the altered perceptions would have been very frightening. The key is to monitor what the person watches and to know your loved one's triggers. If you see signs of agitation (increased breathing, repetitive motion, general upset, etc.), turn off the TV / movie. Instead of watching the news or other programs, play recordings of comedy shows with which the person is familiar (The Carol Burnett Show, Sanford and Son, All in the Family, etc.). Whatever the person enjoyed in times past is usually a good choice, but even these may cause upset for some. Other helpful DVDs are those of familiar music groups. Music and videos are often used by caregivers to calm their loved one during times which might be upsetting to the person or at bad times of the day.

People's Identities: Daniel's father would look at a picture of himself and believe it to be Daniel. One husband chased his wife out of the bed, because he would not sleep with a woman who was not his wife. Ellen's grandfather would have an entire conversation about his son, Wendell, not realizing that he was talking to Wendell at the time. These are all very common behaviors. The person's recognition of others can come, go, and come back again without reason.

The Past: The part of the brain that is most heavily damaged in Alzheimer's disease is the hippocampus, the part where recent memories are stored. Therefore, a person with Alzheimer's disease may remember in great detail the dress she wore to her senior prom 60 years ago, but have no idea what she ate for breakfast 15 minutes ago. This is the hallmark of Alzheimer's disease (the 'save' button on the computer doesn't work anymore). As the disease progresses, even the distant memories may be taken away.

Additionally, your loved one may remember the past as something completely false. Mrs. Smith told her daughter about Mr. Smith's repeated physical abuse, beatings, and injuries --- all things that never occurred. These types of accusations --- the ones that anger and hurt us at the very core of our being --- are the most difficult to ignore. We feel we must argue, correct, reorient. The truth is that this reorientation will not work and very likely will only upset the person. It may be that the caregiver needs a "time out" at this point. It is perfectly acceptable (and probably the best thing you can do) to leave the room, to give yourself time to cool off, to tell yourself yet again that the person is not responsible for her actions. Redirect her if possible with a statement like, "Mom, you know we all love you. Do you remember the time when you and Dad danced at your wedding? That was a happy day!"

The Present: One lady who lived in the same Alzheimer's unit as Ellen's grandmother had been a head nurse at the local hospital for many years. The nursing home looked a great deal like the hospital and this woman believed she was the head nurse of the nursing home unit. She walked around the unit instructing the staff in their duties, addressing issues of cleanliness, etc. Receiving these instructions, the staff members wisely played along with the woman's harmless delusions.

In General: Always keep in mind that the person's perceptions, reasoning, understanding --- EVERYTHING is skewed by this disease. Things that seem irrational to us are very real to them.

Trying to convince them otherwise, rather than soothing their fears, going along with harmless hallucinations or altered perceptions, or distracting / redirecting them, will only cause upset, confusion or agitation in the person and could cause a violent outburst.

Chapter 7

INAPPROPRIATE PUBLIC BEHAVIOR

Of all the difficulties faced by Alzheimer's disease caregivers, inappropriate public behavior is often the most embarrassing and socially isolating for the caregiver. Public toileting, sexual behavior, anger management issues, "hitting" on members of the opposite sex, saying inappropriate things --- the list goes on and on. The potential for embarrassment keeps the caregiver from going out socially and keeps friends and family from issuing invitations to the caregiver, who cannot leave his loved one with Alzheimer's disease by herself. Where does this leave the caregiver? Isolated.

This stage of the disease may last several months or several years, or your loved one may never exhibit these behaviors. How do you cope when these behaviors occur?

First of all, stay calm. Getting angry, blaming your loved one, yelling, or similar reactions will only make things worse. Your mood influences that of your loved one. Reacting rashly will confuse the person, and make it more difficult to stop the behavior.

Try to distract her from the behavior. It may take several tries. Try to find a "hot button" issue that usually distracts your loved one. "Your hair is messed up! You need to go to the restroom and comb it!" or "Let's go get a milkshake!" Find your loved one's "hot button" issue and use it liberally.

For those who try to undress in public or exhibit public sexual behavior, consider a "busy apron" or "Alzheimer's apron," which has buttons, zippers, snaps, etc. all over the front, but fastens in the back. It is just about impossible for a person with Alzheimer's to remove. Several companies offer these online.

One caregiver had business cards printed that said, "My husband has Alzheimer's disease. Please excuse his behavior." Most people will understand if they know why he is acting strangely.

Sometimes, it is most difficult to care for those individuals who have inappropriate behavior in the home. For instance, some people yell all the time. The person may yell at family members or the person may just yell or cry out, not in pain, but as part of the disease process. This is so grating on the nerves of the poor caregiver! Medication may help, but there may be nothing to do but wait for the stage to pass.

Consider Alzheimer's disease daycare for your loved one, so you can keep from being socially isolated. Lester Potts went to a wonderful adult dementia daycare center called Caring Days in Tuscaloosa, Alabama. There he became a watercolor artist. When exposed to art therapy, music therapy, and intellectually stimulating activities, his socially inappropriate behavior improved. Remember that caring for a person with Alzheimer's disease is a marathon, not a sprint. If you do not get respite for yourself, you will not make it to the finish.

If these strategies don't work or are insufficient, talk to your loved one's physician, who may decide medication is necessary.

Chapter 8

CLOTHING

People with Alzheimer's disease often have no understanding of season and temperature, much less how it should affect their clothing choices. Ellen's grandfather wore a toboggan and coat all summer long in his East Tennessee home. Her grandmother could not convince him that he needed to wear clothing appropriate to the weather. He went about their home, which had no air conditioning, closing windows every time she would open them.

Another caregiver picked up his father in the middle of winter to take him to a religious service. Once they arrived, his father took off his overcoat and scarf. To the son's surprise, his dad was wearing nothing on top but a stained, sleeveless undershirt, rather than the sport coat and tie he assumed his father would be wearing.

Wearing clothing inappropriate for the season can be uncomfortable, but wearing clothing inappropriate for the occasion or worse yet, for public view can be embarrassing. As the caregiver, what should you do?

If possible, try not to make clothing a battle. In most people with Alzheimer's disease, this will just make them argumentative and perhaps combative. To prevent problems before they happen, the best thing you can do is to prepare for this situation in advance by controlling the choices. Stated another way, **choose the choices,** so that any item your loved one picks is appropriate. Rotate clothing in the closet and dresser drawers seasonally, so that clothing inappropriate for the season is not available. Some with Alzheimer's will allow their caregivers to display two or three complete outfits from which to choose. If your loved one wants to wear the same outfit every day, buy several inexpensive copies of this outfit, or something so similar that he can't tell the difference.

If your loved one balks at the choices, it may be that he cannot see them. Are the clothes lying on a similarly colored sheet? Those with Alzheimer's lose their ability to discern the differences between similar colors. For instance, a white shirt on light-colored sheets may be "invisible" to him. We cover this concept in more detail later in the book. (see **LIVING SPACES**)

If the person balks at changing clothes at all, simplify the process. Instead of saying, "Let's change your clothes." Go step by step, starting with, "Let's unbutton your shirt" or whatever is appropriate for the articles of clothing he is wearing.

Finally, if you don't like the choice of clothing your loved one makes, ask yourself if it matters. If you are staying at home or going to the grocery store, it probably does not matter. If you are going to your granddaughter's wedding, it does. Strategically choose your battles.

Sometimes, the issue isn't changing clothes, it's keeping clothes on at all. Some people with Alzheimer's disease undress themselves in public. For ladies, you can try dresses or blouses with back zippers or buttons. Usually, these are too complicated for those with Alzheimer's to comprehend. Pullover shirts and blouses also are a good choice. For men, it's more difficult, since the pants are usually the issue. He may need to wear over his clothes a "busy apron" or "Alzheimer's apron," which has zippers, buttons, etc., but is virtually impossible for him to remove. These are also a good option for women and are readily available on the internet.

What do you do when embarrassing moments happen? Take a deep breath, don't panic and react calmly. Try to think of a way to diffuse the situation without embarrassing or berating your loved one with Alzheimer's. Consider the situation mentioned earlier when the father took off his overcoat and was wearing a stained, sleeveless undershirt instead of a coat and tie. His son said, "Wow, dad, this sanctuary is really drafty. I think I'll put my coat back on. Let me help you with yours." Both father and son were able to enjoy the service. No one got upset. The father had no idea he'd done anything wrong, and the son was able to keep the embarrassment to a minimum.

When embarrassing behaviors happen, distraction is always a good idea. Usually, each individual has a distraction that will always work for him. As mentioned earlier, we could always tell Daniel's father, "Your hair is messed up! You need to go comb it!" Immediately, his dad would stop what he was doing, go to the restroom and comb his hair. Most people have a key "distraction phrase" if only you can find it.

For some with Alzheimer's disease, the clothing issue which causes the most difficulty may be related to deteriorating motor skills, not removing clothing in public. As a person loses his mental faculties, he will have increasing problems dealing with things like buttons, zippers, snaps, and other common clothing fasteners. The clothing choices below will make life easier and perhaps keep the person with Alzheimer's disease independent for a longer period of time.

Shoes: Choose Velcro fastened or slip-on shoes. Tying shoe strings is difficult for older hands, even in people without Alzheimer's disease. Clogs or other backless shoes are not a good choice, even as bedroom slippers. They may be comfortable, but your loved one needs the extra support of a shoe back. For ladies, no high (or even moderate-sized) heels. Shoes with gripping soles (sneakers, tennis shoes or something similar) are best for everyone. These are available in a variety of colors, which makes them easier to pair with nicer clothing (think black tennis shoes with a dark suit).

Tops: Pullover shirts work well, unless your loved one has trouble putting her hands over her head. If that is the case, you may need to help with a button or zipper front shirt.

Bottoms: Change to pants and skirts with elastic waists. Many issues with incontinence arise because the person simply can't work their clothing quickly enough.

General Tips: Layered clothing is a good choice. Elderly people, especially those taking blood thinners, are often cold. Unless you are one of those people who love to iron, choose clothing that needs little care. "Wash and wear" needs to be your mantra. Caregiving is difficult enough without adding ironing and dry cleaning to the list of things to do.

Chapter 9

DRESSING / BATHROOM ISSUES

Often "privacy" issues are the ones that provoke the most upset, agitation, and violence in people with Alzheimer's disease. Even those well into the middle or the late stages of the disease still may retain a great sense of modesty.

In general, try to respect the person's privacy and modesty as much as possible. When bathing her, leave her robe on until the last possible minute. In dressing, take one piece of clothing off and replace it with another (replacing one shirt with another, for instance), instead of completely disrobing her and then beginning the dressing process. When giving this kind of very private care, talk about pleasant things the person may remember from the past, play a favorite DVD or music from the person's youth. When bathing, give her a warm washcloth to hold to keep her occupied. Sometimes, the sense of touch helps the person understand what is happening when she otherwise does not understand.

Most bathrooms are equipped with mirrors, but these may confuse the person with Alzheimer's disease and make her believe there is a stranger in the room. Cover the mirrors or take them down. The same holds true for mirrors in the bedroom where you dress the person. If mirrors pose a particular problem, take down or cover all mirrors in the house.

Plan the person's bath at the best time of day for her and make sure she is not hungry at the time.

Blood sugar affects mood. Remember that those with Alzheimer's disease do not get a great deal of exercise and, unless incontinence is an issue, may not need to bathe every day. For safety and ease of use, purchase an electric razor for shaving.

If you have to be somewhere at a certain time, allow plenty of time for a bath and dressing or even bathe her the night before. If you are rushed, your loved one will sense this and it will cause her confusion. Most importantly, if your loved one is becoming violent or agitated, postpone whatever it is that upsets her until later, if possible. You may need to talk to her physician about medication.

As Alzheimer's disease progresses, difficulties controlling bladder and bowel activity begin to occur. Bladder problems usually start first. Your loved one may have trouble understanding that she needs to go to the bathroom, controlling the urge, and walking to the bathroom to get relief. As is discussed later in the **WALKING** section, the parts of the brain that control the bladder are very near those that control the legs, walking, and balance, so these often are affected at the same time. Your loved one's physician may decide to try medications to help control bladder function. Although these may be helpful in some people, they also may have the side effect of worsening memory and causing confusion, so they must be used carefully.

Urinary tract (bladder) infections are very common in those with Alzheimer's disease. Since we know that bladder function is affected by the disease, and the bladder often does not completely empty, it is easy to see why this might be the case. Your loved one also may not be able to recognize or describe to you the common symptoms of a bladder infection, such as burning, pain, a sensation of fullness, the urge to urinate frequently, etc. A urinary tract infection is one of the most common causes of agitation, disruptive behavior, confusion and worsening of physical condition in a person with Alzheimer's disease. Often the urine will look darker and / or cloudy and will take on a very unpleasant smell. Please report to the physician any suspicion you have that your loved one may have a urinary tract infection. Be aware that even in elderly people without Alzheimer's disease, urinary tract or other infections may cause temporary confusion.

Chapter 10

DRIVING ISSUES

Studies show that a frightening number of accidents in the elderly are caused by people with Alzheimer's who should not be on the road in the first place. Since this is such a touchy subject for patients and caregivers alike, those with Alzheimer's disease often continue to drive until they are forced by circumstances to stop. Sometimes, those circumstances are tragic for the person with Alzheimer's disease himself, his passengers, or people in other vehicles. If tragedies are to be prevented, caregivers actively must take responsibility for the situation.

There are many excuses for not addressing the driving issue. "She only drives in her little town," or "I don't think his memory is that bad, do you?" or "He doesn't drive often and NEVER in rush hour!" Excuses aside, the two most common reasons for avoiding this issue are first, the fear of the reaction of the person with Alzheimer's. Family members fear they will be blamed, and their loved one will be angry, hurt, insulted, upset, or depressed. Secondly, the family worries about the added responsibility if the person with Alzheimer's disease cannot drive herself to doctors' appointments, the grocery store, religious services, etc. For these two reasons, people with Alzheimer's disease often drive LONG beyond the point when it is safe.

As a caregiver responsible for a person with Alzheimer's disease, you must be proactive about driving. A Pennsylvania woman with Alzheimer's disease lived alone and still had possession of her vehicle. She was reported missing by a family member, and multiple law enforcement agencies were notified. She had no GPS bracelet (covered later in the book), which would have allowed police to find her soon after she was reported missing. More than 24 hours later, she was found dead in her car. Apparently, she had crossed into New Jersey, had come to a near stop on the New Jersey Turnpike, was struck from behind by an SUV, and struck again by a tractor trailer truck, the force of which pushed her car into a concrete median. This is just one of many horrific stories.

Beyond the cost in human life, the family could be held liable if they knew their loved one had Alzheimer's disease, but did not stop her from driving. Also, insurance coverage may be denied.

Nothing is worth risking precious lives and your family's financial well-being. From personal experience, we can tell you that it is not pleasant to take away a loved one's car keys, but there are some things which may make it easier. First of all, take your loved one for an eye examination. Given the prevalence of cataracts, macular degeneration and other eye conditions in the elderly, your loved one may be forced to give up driving because of sight issues. Make sure the eye doctor knows your loved one has issues with Alzheimer's disease and that the goal is taking away the car keys.

Another alternative is a driving evaluation. If your state does not require a driving evaluation for someone the age of your loved one, ask the physician to order one to be performed by an occupational therapist. This will give you objective information about your loved one's ability to drive.

Lester Potts had this evaluation one year and recognized 17 of 18 road signs. A year later, he recognized 1 of 18 road signs. Our family was flabbergasted. His physician took the keys away from him in the office when he received the test results. If you can find a doctor who will do this, it is an incredible blessing, as it keeps the family from being the "bad guys." If all else fails, see if you can get the employee's of the driver's license bureau involved in keeping your loved one off the roads. People with Alzheimer's (especially men) have been known to take the keys back and drive away.

Often a person with Alzheimer's disease becomes obsessed or fixated on a certain car. If this happens, detach the battery, sell the car, or give the car to a younger member of the family and appeal to your loved one's sense of "helping the younger generation." If it is the car the caregiver drives, keep the keys hidden or around your neck.

Usually (not always), the person will grow accustomed to the idea within a reasonable amount of time and cease to ask about driving. Physician involvement is key if you believe the person will have serious problems giving up the driving. It makes it so much easier for the family to be able to say, "Remember? Here is the paper from Dr. Jones saying that you shouldn't drive anymore." Statements by the caregiver like, "I'll drive today. I need the practice!" are good to keep your loved ones from arguing with you. Eventually, the person stops talking about it. Don't be afraid to be "pushy" or persistent with the doctor about this!

really?

If the person with Alzheimer's manages to take the car out anyway, call the police immediately. Give them the tag number of the vehicle, a likely route (if there is one), and an understanding of the person's condition. If the person has a GPS bracelet (covered later), the police will be able to find him quickly. Calling the police may seem to be a drastic measure, but in doing so, you may save your loved one's life or others.

Remember that driving requires one to make very rapid decisions, considering numerous issues at the same time in a constantly changing situation. Err on the side of caution when considering your loved one's ability to drive safely.

Chapter 11

EATING ISSUES

It seems those with Alzheimer's disease always have eating issues, whether it is eating too much or too little. There usually is not a happy medium.

Eating Too Little:

Of the two eating issues, eating too little is the more difficult to remedy. You can present all kinds of wonderful food, but you cannot force the person to eat. We all can picture the fragile little old lady weighing 90 lbs. soaking wet, the stereotypical malnourished elderly person. Remember that appetite and the lack of appetite are controlled by the brain. If the part of the brain that tells a person she is hungry is affected, she may not want to eat. Additionally, appetite can be affected by depression, usually by creating a lack of appetite, but sometimes by creating excessive appetite. If the person does not want to eat, she may be depressed. Most antidepressants increase appetite, and these medications are often prescribed for people who lack appetite, whether or not they are depressed. Talk to your loved one's physician.

If the person with Alzheimer's disease eats very little, make certain what she does eat is packed with nutrition. Keep healthy snacks around the house, like cut fruit and vegetables. Offer food often.

People with Alzheimer's disease lose their ability to PERCEIVE things the way the rest of us do. Similar colors tend to run together. For instance, if you put mashed potatoes and grilled chicken on a white plate, the person may not understand that there is anything but the plate there. Place the mashed potatoes and chicken on a medium tone plate and suddenly, the food "appears." (In the Alzheimer's disease world, color contrasts are visible, but similar colors placed together may not be visible.) Moreover, patterned plates are confusing to those with Alzheimer's disease. A nice medium tone solid plate is best.

Especially if the person's decrease in appetite is sudden, check her mouth. Ellen's grandmother got thrush, a painful yeast infection of the mouth, which is somewhat common in infants, but not very common in adults. If the person has been on antibiotics, thrush is made more likely. Look for a white film inside the mouth that cannot be dislodged by brushing or scraping. Because this is not very common in adults, it's often missed by healthcare providers. Also, you might check for a cavity, abscessed tooth, jaw disease or dental issues, which make it painful for the person to chew.

If your loved one lives in a facility, make certain she is not placed at the dinner table with someone who is stealing her food. Over-eaters will take food off the plates of people sitting around them.

Swallowing Problems: When the brain of a person with Alzheimer's becomes affected severely enough, difficulty with swallowing is bound to occur and is part of normal disease progression. Also, this may affect your loved one's ability to nourish herself. She literally may "forget" how to eat: the brain cells which control chewing, tongue and cheek movement, throat muscles and coordination of swallowing may have died or lost their connections. The person often begins to "pocket" her food, rather than chewing and swallowing it, and may accumulate large amounts of food in the mouth before trying to swallow. All of this makes aspiration, the spilling of food, liquid or saliva into the windpipe or lungs, more likely. This often begins to happen in the middle stages of the disease, and may become severe in the later stages. In fact, your loved one may become unable to swallow at all in advanced stages. Before this gets to be the case we strongly recommend you discuss feeding options with your loved one's physician. Ideally, this issue should be addressed very soon after the diagnosis of Alzheimer's disease is made as you seek legal assistance with long-term care planning, healthcare directives, living will, etc. Your loved one's wishes regarding nutrition and other issues should be documented and followed while she is still able to make them known.

Speech therapy sometimes may be helpful if your loved one still is able to follow directions. Speak with the physician about this option. Small bites with coaching, sitting straight up, and tucking the chin to swallow may be helpful maneuvers. At some point you may have to make the decision about feeding your loved one artificially (through her veins or with a feeding tube), but ideally, this issue would have been addressed earlier, as discussed above. Although it is hard to do, you should know that withholding nourishment to people with late stage Alzheimer's disease may be the most humane and compassionate thing to do. An interesting case study on this subject entitled *Doing the Right Thing – Helping Families Decide*

Whether to Withhold Artificial Nutrition & Hydration in Alzheimer's Disease, written by Cheryl Pensiero, RN, MS, NP-C, Assistant Professor of Nursing at Columbia University and published in the *Online Journal of Health Ethics*, is available at http://www.ojhe.org/index.php/ojhe/article/viewFile/67/70. Regardless, this decision must be based on your loved one's wishes (if those are known) or yours.

Eating Too Much:

Over-eating is often a problem in people with Alzheimer's disease, and is even more common in some other kinds of dementia, especially fronto-temporal dementia. To a certain extent, one can say that if eating makes the person happy, why worry? However, the weight gain that usually accompanies it can cause back and joint pain, and can increase the person's risk of stroke, heart attack and diabetes. Also, those with Alzheimer's may eat so much that they vomit. Finding a happy medium is key.

First of all, do not serve food "family style" around the table. Daniel's father lost his ability to understand when he should stop eating and gained over 50 pounds as his Alzheimer's disease progressed. He was known to sit down first at the table and eat everything out of several serving bowls before anyone noticed. We learned to keep the food on the stove and serve his plate for him, as it was easier to control portions that way. Do not keep junk food or candy where the person can find it. If he must have snacks, serve fruit, raw vegetables, and other healthy foods that are low in calories and high in nutrition. Individuals with Alzheimer's disease often crave sugars and carbohydrates, and some of the medicines (antipsychotic drugs) used for behavior management increase these cravings.

If the person lives in a facility and eats at a table with others, make certain he is placed with those who will notice and can verbalize if he is stealing their food. This is also true if the person lives at home where there are very young family members. In a rather humorous incident, Lester Potts stole our 3-year-old daughter's rolls off her plate at Christmas dinner, rolls she had been promised as a reward for eating her green beans. Fortunately, she protested this injustice quite loudly, so we knew what had happened.

There are those who overeat, yet are undernourished, because their bodies lose the ability to extract the nutrients and calories out of their food. This was the case with Ellen's grandfather, who would eat a large dinner and five minutes later, swear we were starving him and eat again. He remained unhealthily thin the entire time. Check with the person's physician or a registered dietician about strategies to help keep your loved one nourished.

Above all, do not obsess over food intake. In this as in all things along this journey, caregivers should do the best they can under the difficult circumstances in which they are placed.

Chapter 12

SLEEPLESSNESS

Most people can do anything required of them --- if only they can get a decent night's sleep. If your loved one with Alzheimer's is up several times during the night, this can be the most difficult part of being a caregiver. Ellen's grandmother slept for many years holding the back of her husband's pajama bottoms, so she would know when he got up to wander in the middle of the night. There is no magic cure for this situation, but there are several things you can try (often in conjunction with each other) that may improve your life.

Make certain the person with Alzheimer's disease has NO CAFFEINE whatsoever after mid-afternoon. If this doesn't have an effect, move the "no caffeine" rule back to lunch, then to breakfast, if lunch doesn't work, or perhaps to no caffeine at all. Many teas have more caffeine than coffee. Many soft drinks also have large amounts of caffeine. If your loved one is accustomed to drinking coffee, tea or other caffeinated beverages all day, substitute the decaffeinated version. Energy drinks are full of caffeine and sugar, and should never be given to someone with Alzheimer's disease.

Do not feed your loved one high sugar foods (desserts, candy, non-diet soft drinks, etc.) in the evening. Sugar can agitate people. Remember that bread and other carbohydrates turn into sugar in the bloodstream. If you doubt the effects of sugar, ask any elementary school teacher what the day after Halloween is like!

Try not to allow your loved one to sleep during the day, or no more than a short nap after lunch. Too much sleep during the day means less sleep at night. Also, if you keep the person physically and mentally active all day, she is awake during daylight hours, more tired at the end of the day, and prepared for a good night's sleep. Given before bedtime, warm milk with a little real vanilla extract added may make the person drowsy. Also, there are many de-caffeinated teas available that are recommended for bedtime use.

When your loved one is asleep, does he move frequently? If so, he may have restless leg syndrome, which can keep someone from going into a deep sleep and can awaken them numerous times during the night. If this is the case, there are lifestyle changes and medications that can help. Sleep apnea (think heavy snoring) also can keep a person from falling into a deep sleep. Talk to your doctor about a sleep study.

Note that some medications are prone to keep people awake --- decongestants, steroids, and others. Antihistamines usually make people sleepy, but make some people nervous and wakeful. Check the side effects of the medications your loved one takes with your pharmacist or doctor, and remember to include over-the-counter medications in the discussion.

If these suggestions do not work, or do not work well enough, talk to the doctor about some type of sleep medication. Repeat yet again the mantra of the caregiver: This is a marathon, not a sprint. You must take care of yourself (including getting enough sleep) if you want to finish the race.

Chapter 13

SUNDOWNING

"Sundowning" is a term which refers to the confusion and agitation that often occurs in those with Alzheimer's toward the end of the day. Contributing causes may include late-day fatigue, darkness and shadows, and reduced ability to tolerate stressful situations as the day goes on. Aggravating factors may include pain, caffeine, or sugar intake in the afternoons. If your loved one is in a residential facility, commotion at shift change (usually 3 pm) may be a contributing factor. Wandering, falls, and injuries are all more common during this late afternoon and evening agitation.

Take steps to reduce the likelihood of sundowning. Avoid giving your loved one caffeine and excess sugar and carbohydrates after lunch. Make every effort to keep him stimulated during most of the day in a well-lit environment. Give an early supper with a light snack toward bedtime. Maximize physical and mental activity in the mornings and minimize it at night. Try warm milk with vanilla at bedtime. Always keep a night light burning. Reminisce about familiar, comforting memories late in the day and at night, and try playing soft music. Bring familiar items to your loved one's room if he is in an unfamiliar environment.

Despite these behavioral modifications, your loved may need more aggressive interventions to control his behavior. Certain anti-psychotic medications may be used to help with sundowning. As many of these have serious side effects, they should only be used in cases where other interventions have not proven effective. The medications commonly used to minimize symptoms of Alzheimer's disease also may help to prevent sundowning. In general, these should be prescribed before anti-psychotics are used. Antidepressant medications are sometimes used, as well as tranquilizers and medications often used for seizures. If these measures are not effective, and especially if your loved one becomes violent, he may have to be transported to the emergency room, and from there to an inpatient geriatric psychiatry facility. Other medications can be tried under observation, and your loved one's behavior controlled before being discharged.

Just remember sundowning is an extremely common problem in Alzheimer's disease, but the simple lifestyle changes noted above should go a long way toward calming the person with illness and making life easier on you, the caregiver.

Chapter 14

VIOLENCE

Those with Alzheimer's disease can be violent, especially those whose disease process has affected the main part of the brain that houses judgment (the frontal lobe). People who have been kind, caring human beings all their lives can turn combative and abusive. We have seen this in our own families. Those who retain physical strength longer into the disease process can become a very real danger to their caregivers and others.

What we have noticed is that some people usually can interact without incident with those who have violent tendencies and some people cannot. What is the difference? The techniques we will suggest do not work on everyone, but they work for most people. If you are ever in physical danger, call 911 immediately. If your loved one was given a few minutes of clear-mindedness, he would ask you to do that, too.

First and foremost, if something you are doing is agitating or upsetting your loved one, stop it immediately (unless it's an emergency situation). Know your loved one's physical signs of agitation: increased breathing, franticness, pacing, wringing of hands, etc. When you see your loved one exhibiting these signs, stop whatever you are doing and think of another approach. If you stop, the person usually will calm down to the point where you can deal with him. If he does not and / or you are in physical danger, remove yourself from the situation and call the police. Most people with

Alzheimer's never get to this point, but a small percentage do.

In general, do not argue with those who have Alzheimer's disease. No matter what the person says, find something to agree with or at least manage an "Oh, really?" This is true in all those with Alzheimer's disease, but especially for those with a tendency toward anger and violence. Arguing will only agitate her. Go along with what she says if you can. Redirect her. Smile at her. LOVE her. Gently pat her hand or hug her if it would not be dangerous to do so.

If these techniques do not work, or if they do not control the behavior completely, talk with your loved one's physician about her tendency toward physical aggression. Sometimes, medication is necessary. The doctor may order testing to determine whether the person has another underlying medical condition aggravating her anger management issues.

Blood sugar greatly affects mood and behavior in the elderly. This is doubly true if your loved one has diabetes (high blood sugar) or hypoglycemia (low blood sugar). If you feed your loved one 5 or 6 very small meals a day (or offer healthy snacks between meals), your loved one's blood sugar will stay at a more consistent level. This may improve his behavior. Give the person more protein and less carbohydrates / sweets. Again, the goal is to keep blood sugar at a more consistent level, and protein stays in the bloodstream longer.

If you must do something that you know will upset the person (bathing, doctor's appt, etc.), choose the best time of day for your loved one. Play her favorite music, talk to her about things she enjoyed in years past to keep the person calm through the process ("Remember the time when we were first married and we went...."). It may help to get your loved one some type of music player (iPod, MP3 players, etc.) and earphones to play his favorite music during the upsetting activity, although you cannot use these if the person is bathing.

Be very careful about alcohol consumption. Not only can this interfere with coordination and some medications, but alcohol is a depressant and can affect mood greatly. It also can cause the person balance and coordination problems.

In the worst cases, a person with Alzheimer's disease may have such a tendency toward violence that she has to be committed to a dementia psychiatric facility for the elderly through the court system. This is the last resort, but can be the best solution in a horrific situation. While it is very difficult to stand up and testify that your loved one is a danger to herself and others, a facility of this type may be the only place where she can have her behavior and medication regulated. Talk to an elder law attorney if you feel your loved one may have anger management issues to this degree. We had to pursue this route with Daniel's father.

Chapter 15

WANDERING

This habit of those with Alzheimer's is one of the most potentially dangerous parts of the disease and one of the most terrifying for the caregiver. There are always stories in the news about people with Alzheimer's disease wandering away and never coming back.

Before Ellen's grandfather's descent into Alzheimer's disease, he and her grandmother owned the Western Auto Store in their small town of about 5,000 people in Northeastern Tennessee. Everyone in the area knew them, because they had been customers in the store. With the onset of Alzheimer's disease, he became a wanderer. They lived at the edge of the mountains with cliffs, rivers, creeks and lakes nearby. The potential dangers for him were everywhere, but her family was fortunate. He would wander away relatively often and the neighbors, the police, the townspeople, whoever, would bring him home or call her grandmother to come get him. Many are not so fortunate.

Many caregivers do not take proper precautions against wandering. They believe their loved one will not wander if he has never wandered before. This could be a deadly mistake. Perhaps the person goes to the mailbox and, coming back inside, it's not the house he remembers. To him, it's not his house. Perhaps he goes to the store with his caregiver and wanders away while the caregiver's back is turned. Perhaps the caregiver takes a shower while she believes her loved one is asleep, and he wanders away. Whatever the case, if someone with Alzheimer's disease can walk, he is at risk of wandering.

In the 1970's and early 80's when Ellen's grandfather had Alzheimer's disease, there were very few options available to prevent wandering. Now, things have changed dramatically. There is a wonderful non-profit organization called Project Lifesaver International with partners around the country. Through these partners, they provide GPS bracelets, not just to those with Alzheimer's disease, but to anyone at risk of wandering --- those with autism, Down Syndrome, and other types of cognitive impairment. To date, well over 2,000 successful rescues have been performed with a 100% success rate. Go to their website (www.projectlifesaver.org) for more information. People always are concerned that the Alzheimer's disease patient will remove the bracelet. In our community, out of the hundreds distributed, only one person has been able to successfully remove it. Also, if Project Lifesaver is not available in your area, there are other organizations and companies that supply devices like these. Check with your local senior center, Alzheimer's support group, or local law enforcement. In our area, Project Lifesaver is administered through the county sheriff's department and Caring Days Adult Daycare Center. Even for those living in a locked residential care facility, we recommend they wear a GPS bracelet. It is not uncommon for residents to escape, even in facilities with excellent security. We do not recommend the notification systems where the person wears a transmitter around his neck and is required to press a button to call for help, because those with Alzheimer's disease may not have the mental capacity to perform this task, especially in a crisis.

A GPS bracelet is an essential tool to help find someone with Alzheimer's disease if she wanders away, and no ambulatory person with dementia should be without one. However, there are many precautions you can take to prevent wandering before it happens. Use door knob covers (found in the child-proofing sections of stores like Target and Wal-Mart). Most of those with Alzheimer's disease are not able to understand them well enough to exit the home. Install keyed deadbolt locks (keeping the key around your neck for fire safety). If a person is at a stage in the disease process at which he could not exit the home in an emergency (think fire), he should NEVER be left at home alone. The deadbolt locks should only be used when a caregiver with the key is present.

In the chapter of this book entitled "Living Spaces," we cover simple things you can do with decor which can help prevent wandering. For instance, paint doorways and doorknobs leading outside the same colors as the walls to camouflage them. Continue wallpaper borders across the doors. Place large, red "STOP" signs over doors you don't wish the person to use. Place large, black floor mats in front of doorways you don't wish the person to use. Often, those with Alzheimer's believe this is a hole.

Much as you wish to include your loved one in outings, avoid taking her places where you may be distracted --- grocery shopping, clothes shopping, etc. Your loved one could wander away while you are distracted. Ask any parent who has ever lost a child in a store. It can happen in an instant. This has happened in our family, and it is very frightening.

Again, take the car keys away. This may be the most important thing you can do overall. It is one thing to find a person who has wandered away on foot. It's quite another to try to find a person who has wandered away in a vehicle that can travel at high rates of speed.

Chapter 16

WALKING AND BALANCE PROBLEMS

As Alzheimer's disease progresses, it not only affects your loved one's mental condition, but also her physical condition. The person's body becomes less able to perform the activities you and I take for granted, like walking, swallowing, going to the bathroom, etc. This is because the parts of the brain that control these activities become damaged by the illness and lose their connections with other nerve cells. For instance, the nerve cells which control the legs and the bladder are very near each other in the frontal lobes of the brain, so they often become affected at nearly the same time in the disease course. In addition, other conditions which may be present in older people, like vision problems, arthritis and inner ear disease may contribute to poor balance.

As you observe your loved one, you may begin to notice that his walking looks different. It may become slower, more stooped, and more careful. He may begin to hesitate when he first starts out or changes directions. Turns may become more difficult, and he may lose balance when turning, standing up, leaning over or sitting down. His steps may take on a "shuffling" quality, similar to those of a person with Parkinson's disease. You may have to steady and guide him, even down familiar paths. Falls become much more likely during this time, usually in the middle stages of the illness. This is all part of the normal progression of Alzheimer's disease.

Unfortunately, there is nothing that will reverse these changes. However there are steps that should be taken to lower your loved one's risk of falling. For instance, look carefully at the floors in your home and make sure they are cleared of clutter and objects that could trip or confuse your loved one, like stray clothes or shoes, throw rugs, and spilled liquids or powders. Rugs with patterns are particularly confusing to those with Alzheimer's. If you have steps or stairs in the home, try to make these inaccessible to your loved one, except at times when you or another caregiver is present to help him up or down them. If the use of stairs is necessary, make sure sturdy rails are present.

Falls often occur in the bathroom when the person is sitting on or arising from the toilet, or getting in or out of the tub or shower. Installing tub and commode rails, shower chairs, and rubber mats can help reduce fall risk. It is essential that the floor of the bathroom be kept dry. Your loved one should not be allowed to walk in sock feet, but should wear comfortable, supportive shoes with gripping soles that are easy to place and remove from the feet (see **CLOTHING** section). Steps to prevent **WANDERING** are also necessary, and are covered in that section. Along those lines, walking on uneven ground should be avoided if possible. If it is unavoidable, you should steady your loved one carefully to keep him from falling. It often only takes the touch of a hand on a wall, cane, walker, rail or a caregiver to steady someone and keep them from falling.

If your loved one is not so advanced that he cannot follow directions, then gait and balance training with an experienced physical therapist may be helpful in preventing falls. Home health agencies often offer this type of therapy, which has the advantage of being covered by most insurance companies and Medicare. Be sure to ask your loved one's physician about this option.

If a fall should happen, call 911 and have the paramedics perform an assessment on your loved one and help get him up safely. Injuries may occur to both the caregiver and to your loved one if you try and do this yourself. **Be careful**!

Chapter 17

SEVERE WEATHER

Many caregivers are faced with the difficult task of caring for their loved one during and after severe weather. In general, the elderly fare poorly in severe weather and are in particular danger. They are less "techno-savvy," so they have less access to information and warning devices, such as NOAA weather radios, smart phones and computers. Many are hard of hearing and do not hear tornado sirens. If the power or cable television goes out, they may be cut off from all advanced warning. Added to this, about half of all those 85 and above have at least mild dementia. This population may not be able to think and act quickly.

To keep those with dementia safe, plan ahead. If you hear that severe weather is coming and your loved one lives alone or with another elderly person, bring the person(s) to your home, and bring all medications with you in case they are needed. If a warning is issued for your area, the place of greatest safety is the smallest room on the lowest floor in the center of the home, away from doors and windows. Often, this place is an interior hall, closet or bathroom. If it is a closet, clear enough room in advance for everyone in the home to take cover. Note that elderly people have trouble getting up and down off the floor. You may need to move a chair in your safe room. If you live in a mobile home, go to a local shelter.

For those with dementia, everything is made more complicated. Your loved one will sense your agitation and fear, so try to stay calm. Many balk at going into a closet or other safe place. Try to calmly talk them into moving to safety. If the person still refuses, make it into a game, perhaps hide and seek where the two of you hide. Break the process of getting into your safe place into the smallest possible steps. Especially under stress, people with dementia often refuse to do things, because they cannot remember how to do them. Instead of saying, "There's a tornado warning. Let's get in our safe place," say instead, "Let's stand up. Now let's walk across the room. See this closet? It is the safest place for us now. Can you walk into the closet? Thank you. Can you sit in the chair?" Whatever the scenario, break it into the smallest possible steps whenever possible. If the person still refuses, you need to be in the safe place. Danny's father with Alzheimer's disease would sit outside the closet, while Danny's mother sat inside.

While you remain in your safe place, a person with dementia may want to leave before the "all clear" is given. To pass the time, sing familiar songs together. Choose songs from the person's teens and twenties or if the person is religious, familiar hymns. Tell stories. Play games. Anything to keep the person from leaving the safe place.

If the person with dementia loses his home or has his home damaged by severe weather, expect much greater confusion than usual.

CHAPTER 18

"DO YOU REMEMBER ME?"

For most people living with Alzheimer's disease, the time comes when they may have trouble remembering loved ones, may not remember them consistently or may not remember them at all. For all those who love the person, this is one of the most horrific parts of the disease. Deep down in all of us who have been in that position, there is a part that screams, "If you love me, how could you forget me?" It is one of the worst realities of Alzheimer's disease for both those who have it and those who love them.

For most, but not all, this stage comes. Of all our relatives with Alzheimer's disease, only Daniel's father did not lose recognition of loved ones, or at least, he lost his language function long before he lost is ability to recognize us. He might not have remembered us toward the end of his life, but he could not *verbalize* that he did not remember us. Somehow, that made it easier. Preparing for this stage can soften the blow, if it ever comes.

"Do you remember me?" As two people who have supposedly normal memories, but have trouble remembering names, this question places us in a very uncomfortable position. The case is no different for someone living with Alzheimer's disease. You begin the conversation with a test that sets up the person for failure. Instead, change the dynamics of the situation entirely in your approach.

If you live with the person with Alzheimer's disease, announce arriving guests and mention a connecting event which may help jog your loved one's memory. "Darling, here is your granddaughter, Ellen, who has come from Huntsville to see you." Wait for some type of reaction from your loved one, as it takes someone with Alzheimer's more time to process information. Once the reaction comes, whether your loved one remembers the person or not, add a reference to some happy connecting event from the relatively distant past. "Remember when you taught her to fish?" If you are a visitor, introduce yourself in the same way. This may serve as an introduction to conversation.

In general, do not test the memories of people with Alzheimer's disease. Quizzing your loved one may make her feel inadequate. Always phrase things to make your loved one feel capable and good about herself, even when he makes a mess, says or does something wrong, etc. "I have that same trouble myself!" or "I am SO bad with names!" Validating others is important for any human relationship, but for people living with Alzheimer's (many of whom recognize their dwindling capabilities), it is absolutely essential.

Chapter 19

DEPRESSION

In the early to middle stages of the disease, most people with Alzheimer's know they are losing their memories or at least know that something is not right. Depression is a very common side-effect. Because depression can mimic Alzheimer's disease or make it worse, caregivers need to do everything they can to minimize this problem. There are two basic approaches, behavioral treatment and medical treatment, both of which are summarized here.

What is depression and what are the symptoms?

Dictionary.com defines it as "a condition of general emotional dejection and withdrawal." Depression is not something to be embarrassed about or ashamed of. It has a chemical basis in the brain. Some symptoms experienced by people with depression are anxiety; sadness; lack of smiling, laughing, or enjoyment; irritability, annoyance, short temperedness; agitation, restlessness, hand wringing, or hair pulling; multiple physical complaints or hypochondria; disinterest in usual activities; eating more or less than usual; weight loss or gain; lack of energy; sleeping more or less than is normal; feeling that life is not worth living, suicidal wishes, or making a suicide attempt; self-deprecation, self-blame, poor self-esteem, and feelings of failure and worthlessness; pessimism or anticipation of the worst possible outcome.

According to numerous studies, depression is very common among those with Alzheimer's disease and is very much under-diagnosed by physicians. We have found this to be very true in our own experiences. Be an advocate for the person for whom you are caring. If you are concerned your loved one may be depressed, talk seriously about it with the physician.

Behavioral Methods of Avoiding Depression

Interestingly enough, the behavioral issues covered in this section are *those of the caregiver, not the person with Alzheimer's disease.* It would do no good to ask the person with Alzheimer's disease to change his behavior. Caregiver behavior is the key.

How do you interact with the person with Alzheimer's? The first thing to learn is that you cannot bring him into the real world, so do not try. This is an especially difficult lesson for family members, who have known the person for many years as a logical, intelligent member of society. Family members believe that if they can just "reorient" the person long enough, perhaps they can bring back the person they knew. However, constantly correcting the person only contributes to depression and feelings of low self-worth. In her book, Learning to Speak Alzheimer's, Joanne Koenig Coste states, "The person [with Alzheimer's] may soon forget what you say, but they will never forget how you made them feel."[4]

---

[4] Learning To Speak Alzheimer's, Joanne Koenig Coste, Houghton – Mifflin, 2003, p. 50

Consider this scenario: Each day home health nurse visited Miss Ruth, a very elderly woman with Alzheimer's disease. When the nurse arrived, Miss Ruth would say with a big smile on her face, "I had breakfast with my mother this morning." Every morning, the nurse would correct Miss Ruth saying, "Ma'am, your mother has been dead for many years." Predictably, tears and grief followed. In Miss Ruth's mind, her mother died anew every day. As the day wore on, Miss Ruth might not remember the exact words or that her mother was dead, but the *feeling of sadness* remained.

This is an extreme example of what not to do. However, when we constantly correct the person with Alzheimer's disease, we reinforce her view of her own inadequacies. In most cases, correction is not the necessary or kind response. The alternative is to love the person where she is, to validate the abilities she still has, to help her find abilities she may not have had before his diagnosis.

Consider the story of Lester Potts, who could repair just about anything before he got Alzheimer's disease. As symptoms of Alzheimer's became more apparent, he was aware of his own dwindling capabilities, and so became depressed. He stopped smiling and grew frustrated with his own inept attempts to accomplish tasks. After he lost the ability to hammer a nail or change a light bulb, he began attending Caring Days, a local adult daycare center for those with memory disorders. Here, he was exposed to art and music therapy. He learned to paint beautiful watercolors, although he had never painted anything more artistic than a wall or a fence before his diagnosis. By the time of his death, he had painted nearly 100 water colors which have been exhibited all over the country. (To watch a video of some of Lester's art, go to http://www.youtube.com/watch?v=I6ksfsp94YQ. After he began painting, he regained his smile and took tremendous pride in his artistic ability. Music therapy was equally beneficial. He could not sing in tune before the diagnosis of Alzheimer's disease, but afterward, he had a lovely singing voice and sang in tune until the day of his death, even though he did not speak in the last several months of his life.

Good adult daycare can be invaluable in avoiding depression. In addition to granting respite to the caregiver, it gives a person with Alzheimer's a purpose for getting up in the morning, and gives her mentally stimulating activities all day. If you do not have access to good adult daycare (SEE **RESPITE CARE**), try to recreate this environment at home as much as you can. Help the person find something she can do, which may or may not be something she did before her diagnosis. Crafts, charity projects, art, music --- all these are valuable tools in the fight against depression. Especially when doing crafts or art, remember that a perfect end product is not the goal. The goal is to provide cognitively stimulating activity and to make the person feel good about herself. Criticism of any kind should not enter into the equation.

Give the person something to do that she believes contributes to the family or the community. For instance, one woman with Alzheimer's loved to fold and unfold clothing. Her daughter gave her a large laundry basket of old clothes to fold. It kept her mother busy for a long while and made her mother feel like she had contributed to the family. Clients at Caring Days Adult Daycare do all kinds of simple charity projects --- assembling care baskets for

AIDS patients, making wreaths and other crafts to raise money for their new building, etc. Everyone wants to be a contributing member of society. Help those with Alzheimer's disease contribute in ways that work for them.

Keep things fun! Enjoyable activities are valuable tools for both caregivers and those with Alzheimer's disease to avoid depression. Sing, dance, exercise, and be silly. Have fun!

Medical Treatment of Depression

Sometimes, behavioral changes are not enough to combat depression and medication is necessary. As the caregiver, if you see symptoms that concern you (especially those noted earlier), document the symptoms, give a description, and note the frequency and duration over a couple of weeks. Bring this to the doctor's appointment. If you do not feel comfortable talking about this issue in the examination room in front of the person with Alzheimer's, send the physician a letter or e-mail detailing the information at least a few days BEFORE the visit, so the physician has time to review it.

Sudden changes in mood can be a result of medication changes, blood sugar issues, or other medical problems. These possibilities need to be considered as part of the medical evaluation.

If your loved one's doctor recommends medication, please note that the newest medication on the market may not be the best. Different antidepressant medications work in different ways and help some symptoms more than others.

Additionally, the person with Alzheimer's may be on other medications which could negatively interact with some antidepressants. Make certain to take a list of the medications the person is taking and the dosages to the doctor's appointment (always important regardless). The doctor will consider all these things before prescribing an antidepressant. An older, less expensive medication available in generic form may be the best alternative for many people.

Understand that antidepressants take up to several weeks to reach their full potency in the body. Do not expect immediate results. Also, medications work differently in different people. The doctor may have to try several different antidepressants over a period of months to find the one that works best.

If the person with Alzheimer's disease is placed on an antidepressant, keep a log (like the one recommended earlier) documenting the symptoms, frequency, duration, etc. Compare it to the log made before the time when she began the medication. If you are concerned about the medication's effectiveness after the period of time when the doctor said it ought to have reached full potency, send a letter / e-mail to the doctor a couple of days before the visit and begin again. (By the way, this documentation technique is excellent for any medical problem.)

Finally, antidepressant medications are not the silver bullet we would all like them to be. They do not necessarily cure the symptoms of depression completely, but they are invaluable tools to combat depression in those with Alzheimer's disease and others. Just like regulating anything else --- blood sugar, blood pressure, etc. --- it takes time to find what works for each person. Be patient.

Caregiver Depression

Caregivers are also at great risk for depression, given their circumstances, especially those who have no respite care available. In Daniel's neurology practice, he often sees caregivers who spend the entire office visit crying. They literally have no one else to talk to, no help, and no respite. If this describes you or if you have some of the symptoms of depression noted above, please get help. Talk to your physician about your situation and your circumstances. This is especially true if you are having feelings of hopelessness. There have been desperate caregivers who became so depressed they harmed their loved ones or committed suicide themselves. If you believe you may be depressed, break the cycle by talking with a physician or counselor immediately. You are only human. You must take care of your own needs, so that you may be the most effective caregiver possible.

Chapter 20

GOOD NEWS, BAD NEWS

As is often the case in life, there are no hard and fast answers regarding what kind of news to share with someone who has Alzheimer's and what not to share. Here is an example of what we mean: John has Alzheimer's disease and is in the middle stage. John's high school age grandson, Blake, has been diagnosed with cancer. Should John be told?
There is no right or wrong choice in situations such as these. It's a judgment call for John's family. In this case, Blake lives several hours away from John and does not see him often. Also, John promptly forgets anything he is told. John's family decided not to tell him about Blake's cancer diagnosis, reasoning that John would forget anyway, and that if he remembered or had a lingering feeling, it would be negative. We concur with their decision. If Blake had been chosen president of the student body or captain of the football team, our recommendation would be entirely different. If John remembered or had lingering feelings about one of these announcements, they would be positive.

What if Blake lived nearby and saw his grandfather every day, or what if Blake visited John while he was being treated for cancer? John might notice the hair loss from chemotherapy or other side effects. In this case, the family might choose to tell John something of Blake's condition, especially if John asks about it. "Blake has been ill and has had to take some treatment. He's feeling better now than he was." If John has questions, the family should answer them using their best judgment on what John is capable of understanding.

As mentioned earlier in this book, there are many cases where those with Alzheimer's disease do not remember that a family member or friend has died. Their caregivers, struggling with their own grief, must listen to frequent questions about the deceased or even may be mistaken for the deceased. This is horrific. However, telling the person with Alzheimer's over and over that his loved one is dead will only add to the difficulties. Respite care is always essential, but is especially important when the caregiver is struggling with illness or grief in other areas of her life.

In general, we recommend erring on the side of sharing good news and withholding bad, unless it cannot be avoided.

Chapter 21

LIVING SPACES

Interior Decor

It may seem strange that decor would matter to a caregiver, but it can have an enormous effect on the safety and independence of a person with Alzheimer's disease. Additionally, well-structured living space actually can bolster the sense of "self" in someone with Alzheimer's disease. As the illness progresses, it may cause the person to have visual perception (not necessarily sight) problems. Often, people with Alzheimer's can see perfectly well, *but the way their brains interpret what they see malfunctions.* (This is also important to remember when considering driving abilities. See **DRIVING ISSUES**.)

As time goes on, many people with Alzheimer's disease lose their ability to distinguish things of similar color tone from one another. As the caregiver, you can use this knowledge to help the person maintain her independence longer and to help keep her safe. THE KEY is color --- highlighting those things you want the person to notice with contrasting colors and camouflaging those things you do not want her to notice with similar tones.

If the wall behind the commode and sink is painted a similar color, the commode and sink may be "invisible" to the person with Alzheimer's. This is also true if the wall behind the sink or commode is covered in a patterned wallpaper. Paint the wall behind the sink and commode a contrasting color and the sink and commode become "visible" again, perhaps allowing the person to maintain his bathroom independence longer.

If you place light colored food (mashed potatoes, corn, light colored meats like chicken, etc.) on a light colored plate, or dark colored food (like beef or spinach) on a dark colored plate, the food may be invisible to the person. Place food on a contrasting colored plate and the person may be able to maintain her independence in eating longer. If you fill a clear glass with water, the person may not be able to see it. Use a cup in a contrasting color instead. Watch your tablecloth or placemat colors. Make certain the plate and cup do not blend in with the background. Also, patterns tend to confuse those with Alzheimer's disease. A patterned plate or tablecloth may keep the person from eating.

Dark-colored clothes on a dark bedspread or light colored clothes on light-colored sheets may keep the person from being able to dress herself.

On the floor, a shiny finish (polished tile or highly polished wood) may look like water or ice to the person, and make her afraid to walk on the floor. Dull finishes are best. Again, avoid bold patterns in general on the furniture and floor, just as on your plates. A patterned carpet or oriental rug may make it appear that the floor is covered in snakes. To help maintain bathroom independence at night, place reflector tape on the floor from the person's bed to the bathroom and use a nightlight. However, be aware that shadows can be frightening to people with Alzheimer's. During waking hours, try to minimize shadows and make lighting mimic sunlight.

Decor and Wandering Precautions

You can also use color to help keep the person safe. If you paint doors and door knobs the same color as the wall --- or even continue a wallpaper border across a door painted the same color as the wall --- the person with Alzheimer's may not perceive that the door is there at all, reducing the risk of wandering. For public buildings, check local fire codes. However, this is fine for private homes.

Often, a large black floor mat in front of a door will look like a dark hole to a person with Alzheimer's disease, and the person will not walk across it. Many people place black mats in front of doors leading outside to keep their loved ones from exiting the home. Another technique you can use to keep a person with Alzheimer's from wandering outside is to place a traffic "STOP" sign on the inside of exterior doors. Often the color, word or shape --- one of the three or the combination of the three --- will reach the person's mind and keep her from exiting through the door.

Remember, just as with most issues with Alzheimer's disease, visual perception issues may come and go. The person is not "faking" or missing things visually to spite the caregiver. It is another quirk of the disease process. Remember this also when evaluating driving ability (see **DRIVING ISSUES**).

Exterior Spaces

One of the best things you can do for the health and attitude of those with Alzheimer's disease is to give them a secure outdoor area where they can garden, exercise, and enjoy fair weather. Just like interior spaces, though, exterior spaces need to be modified to suit the unique needs of a person with Alzheimer's disease.

Start with a high, opaque fence. Wide open spaces, passing traffic, and other distractions may be upsetting to those with Alzheimer's disease. Make certain the gate is locked. Get advice from a landscape designer or horticulturalist on the plants in your outdoor area to make certain none of them are poisonous. Also, thorny plants (roses, holly bushes, pyracantha, etc.) are not good choices for those with Alzheimer's disease as they may cause injury.

Especially if your loved one enjoyed gardening previously, designate space for planting annuals. If the person has trouble getting up and down, consider window boxes for planting annuals or vegetables.

Add comfortable benches or gliders to sit and enjoy pleasant weather. Rocking chairs can tip. On patios, ceiling or other fans can make an uncomfortably warm day pleasant.

Gardening can give those suffering from Alzheimer's disease a sense of accomplishment and of contributing to the family. You can encourage these positive feelings by phrasing gardening suggestions in a positive light: "Would you please help me plant some pansies? You are so much better at arranging them than I am," or "I really need your help getting this garden into shape. The weeds have taken over!"

A word about swimming pools: Pools are a danger to those with Alzheimer's disease. Those who have been swimming all their lives may get into the pool (or fall into the pool) and forget how to swim. The perception problems of Alzheimer's disease make it doubly dangerous. For someone with Alzheimer's disease who remembers how to swim, he may step into the pool by accident, misjudging the distance, depth, etc. Even if the person usually does not venture outside, the risks of head injury and drowning are too great not to take precautions. Pool supply stores sell fences just for the area around the pool. Also, these are available over the internet.

For more detailed information about interior and exterior environmental design for those Alzheimer's disease, we recommend the book, I'm Still Here, by John Zeisel, Ph.D. who is a noted expert in the field.

General Safety in the Home:

There are more dangers in the home for those with Alzheimer's than could possibly be covered in one book. Seemingly innocent things can cause serious injury to people or property and even loss of life. Safeguarding your home for someone with Alzheimer's is a similar process to childproofing your home for a toddler. The same general principles apply. Look around your home, especially in the areas between hand and eye level of the person with Alzheimer's. What might the person access that could be of danger? In the earliest stages, this does not apply particularly, but as the person progresses, unless your loved one cannot walk and is not able to push himself in a wheelchair, Alzheimer's-proofing your home is of paramount importance.

First and foremost, take all firearms and ammunition out of the house as early as possible in the disease process. As a little girl, Ellen remembers her grandfather, George Chapman, showing her a pistol he got from an uncle many years before. As is often the case with Alzheimer's sufferers, he became fixated on a few objects and the stories he remembered that surrounded those. The gun was one of those objects. It was not loaded, and presumably the bullets had been taken out of the house, but people outside the family would not have known Mr. Chapman was not brandishing a loaded pistol at them. He was a wanderer. He easily could have taken the pistol as he wandered away and provoked a tragedy.

Secondly, go through the home looking for anything that could cause injury --- knives, scissors, matches, kerosene heaters, lighters, etc. --- and put them where the person with Alzheimer's cannot access them. This also holds true for small objects that can be swallowed. For electric stoves, have an electrician install a hidden switch where the power to the stove is cut off. For gas stoves and gas logs, call the gas company about installing safety precautions for these items. Many people with Alzheimer's disease cause a fire by trying to cook something and forgetting it is on the stove. In our own home, we can turn on the gas starter for the fireplace without lighting it. This would be a huge danger to someone with Alzheimer's.

Any type of acetylene torch, welding torch, or other incendiary devices should be sent elsewhere. The same holds true with power tools --- drills, saws, electric hedge clippers, etc. Long after Daniel's father should not have been using power tools, he seriously cut Daniel's mother's hand by accident while trying to trim the hedges with electric trimmers.

Cover electrical outlets with plastic outlet covers. Cover exterior doorknobs with those designed for child-proofing. Replace interior doorknobs that lock with those that do not.

For bathroom safety, set hot water heater temperatures at no greater than 120°F to make certain the person cannot scald himself with hot water. Install grab bars, shower seats, and non-skid mats on the floor and in the floor of the shower or tub. Before you bathe someone with Alzheimer's, make certain to have all you need for the task beside the tub or shower. When an Alzheimer's patient looks at himself in the mirror, he may see a stranger or someone frightening. This is particularly true when the person is being bathed and already feeling vulnerable. You may need to cover the mirrors or remove them, not only in the bathroom and bedroom, but also in the rest of the house if your loved one has a particular problem with mirrors.

Rationalizing that the person is never alone, many caregivers do not "Alzheimer's proof" their homes. "I'm always with him." Do you take him with you when you bathe or go to the bathroom? Do you walk to the mailbox without him to get the mail? Have you ever gone to another room when you thought he was asleep? Do you ever sleep yourself? If the answer to any of these questions is "yes" and the person with Alzheimer's can walk, he is at risk of being harmed by the things described above.

Chapter 22

DENIAL

Ellen's grandfather, George Chapman, began noticing memory issues in his early sixties. It took a couple of years before those became severe enough for him and her grandmother to sell their store and retire. In the early 1970's, most people had not heard of Alzheimer's disease, nor was it a term commonly used by most physicians, even though Dr. Alois Alzheimer named the condition in 1901. "Hardening of the arteries" was the usual term to describe any type of memory issues. Her grandmother and parents took Mr. Chapman to Emory University in Atlanta where he was diagnosed with Alzheimer's disease in about 1974.

As a child Ellen remembers being sent out to walk with her grandfather in the yard to keep him from wandering away and to give her grandmother some respite. However, some of her most vivid memories before the visit to Emory are of the conversations that occurred in the car as she and her family were leaving the Chapmans' house for the 6 hour drive home. "Don't you think he was better this time?" her mother would say. Her father would agree, probably just to be kind. Her mother would give examples of things Ellen's grandfather had done that indicated he was "better" than the last visit. After the trip to Emory, there was no denial possible. Although her family did not know the specifics, they knew the generalities from what the doctor had said. "Better" was not ever going to happen.

Some version of this story has been the case in nearly every family dealing with Alzheimer's disease. You want to explain away the forgetfulness, the declining abilities, and the confusion. There usually comes a point when your denial is forcibly stripped away. This was certainly the case in both our families.

Family members leave denial behind at different times and in different ways. When my denial is stripped away, it is easy for me to grow frustrated with those who are still in denial. Why can they not see the obvious symptoms? Love and other emotions blind people to the reality of the situation.

For those in denial: If people repeatedly tell you about your loved one's memory issues, listen to them. Don't "shoot the messenger."

For those recently shocked out of denial: Do not feel guilty because you failed to see your loved one's cognitive issues clearly. It would be a challenge to find someone who has not been in denial who is in your situation. Do not be so hard on yourself.

For those trying to get someone out of denial: Be kind, gentle and understanding. Everyone processes this type information differently. Eventually, it will be impossible for them to remain in denial. Give the person time.

Chapter 23

CAREGIVER GUILT

Was there ever a more dedicated, yet guilt-filled lot than family caregivers? On the one hand, the caregiver feels guilty for not spending more time with his loved one with Alzheimer's disease, so he spends more time with her. Then, he feels guilty because he is neglecting his work and family, so he increases the time spent there. The cycle begins again. Other common guilt triggers: placing your loved one in a residential facility, placing your loved one in your home, taking over daily tasks from your loved one, leaving your loved one daily tasks that frustrate and depress her, going behind your loved one's back to do things that must be done, confronting your loved one about things that must be done only to have her argue angrily with you....

The list goes on and on. The common thread here is that caregivers cannot win for losing. They second guess themselves and undervalue the gift they are giving their loved ones at every turn.

First of all, value your gift. You are giving the best you can to your loved one. You are not the perfect caregiver, but then, no one is. Give as much grace to yourself as you would to someone else in the same situation.

Second, realize that you have to take care of yourself to be an effective caregiver. If you are always giving to your loved one with Alzheimer's disease and to your family, you will have nothing left for yourself and you will burn out. At the risk of being repetitive, caregiving is a marathon, not a sprint.

Third, understand that in all likelihood, you will make decisions you said you would never make. "I promised Mama I would never put her in a nursing home," or "I promised Daddy I would never lie to him," or "I promised my husband he could die at home." These and a thousand other promises were made when you were not in the real situation, faced with a small array of really poor choices. Do your best to keep your promises, but realize that you may be forced to make other choices for the good of everyone concerned, not just your loved one with Alzheimer's disease.

Stop comparing yourself to others. "Sue kept her mother at home for 10 years. How can I even think of putting my father in a nursing home after only a month?!!" Your situation is not the same as the other caregiver's. Your loved one with Alzheimer's disease has different needs and causes different problems than the other caregiver's. Furthermore, your circumstances are different. Make decisions based on what is best for you, your family, and your loved one, not based on what another caregiver chose to do.

"Lily has done so much for me and cared for me after my surgery. I should be able to drop everything and care for her!" No, you should not. You should do whatever your circumstances reasonably allow to help Lily, but there is no great scorekeeper in the sky who keeps up with the points Lily has amassed vs. you as her caregiver.

One of the main reasons we wanted to write this book is because of the mistakes we and other family members made in caring for our loved ones, simply because we did not have the tools to know better. In caregiving as in everything else in life, there is great need of an ability to forgive yourself and others.

Forgive yourself. Love yourself. Have faith in yourself. Do the best you can under very difficult circumstances, knowing full well that you will fail to meet your own standards on a regular basis.

Chapter 24

LYING TO THOSE WITH ALZHEIMER'S DISEASE

The thought of lying to our loved ones with Alzheimer's disease gives us great pause, as most of us strive to be truthful people. It also causes tremendous guilt. However, there are situations with Alzheimer's disease where you should choose to lie FOR THE GOOD of your loved one. Those with Alzheimer's disease cannot come into your world, so you must enter theirs. For instance, a lady with Alzheimer's disease in a nursing home was very upset that a cat under her bed had birthed kittens. She reported this to the nurse. Of course, the nurse saw no cat or kittens under the bed. However, she wisely told the lady that she would take the cat and kittens out of the room and find them a good home. The nurse calmly bent underneath the bed, gathered the imaginary feline family, and took them out of the room. The lady was relieved and happy, rather than upset and argumentative as she would have been if the nurse had tried to contradict her. There are a million situations like this, most of which do not involve hallucinations. Just as when you have an imaginary tea party with imaginary cups and tea, you are not lying to the child. You are entering her world. You must do the same for those with Alzheimer's disease.

Remember Miss Ruth, who believed she had breakfast with her mother every morning? The home health nurse told her every day that her mother was dead, which caused Miss Ruth to grieve her mother's death anew in her mind and heart.

Most of us would agree that the nurse chose legalism over kindness and compassion in Miss Ruth's case. If the nurse had said, "Really? What did you talk about? What did you have to eat?" She would not have been lying, just asking Miss Ruth questions about the morning as Miss Ruth remembered it.

"I had breakfast with my mother today," when you know her mother is dead. "You need to take me home now," when he is home. "I've already had my bath," when you can smell that she has not. "The people in the next room are having a party," when you are in the house alone with him. How do you respond? The best way to respond is to choose kindness over truthfulness, compassion over being correct, love over being right.

"You need to take me home now." Your father is home, but it is not the home he recognizes. There is no home he recognizes, so you respond, "Yes, dad, I'll take you home. I just need to finish a few things first. While you're here, would you help me with...." Make your father feel useful, like he is a productive member of the family. Help him find something familiar through looking at old pictures or something else he enjoys. Distract him from the need to go home. Unfortunately, it may be that the distraction only lasts for a few minutes before he asks again. Art and music may be helpful choices at this point. Daniel's father could concentrate on art for long periods of time, when concentrating on anything else was beyond him.

"I've already had my bath." Your mother has not had her bath, but you respond, "You're right. Would you mind if I change your shirt, though? I think there is a spot on it and I want to put it in the wash before it stains." Then, do the same with her pants. Ask her to hold a warm washcloth, lead her to the tub. Tell her that, since the bath water is already run, she might as well take a bath. Because something involving multiple steps like taking a bath may be intimidating and confusing, break everything down into the very smallest steps.

"There are people in the next room who are having a party." What should your reply be? "Should we join them?" or "Good heavens! It sounds really wild!" or "Yes, but I will ask them to keep it down, since you're ready for bed."

There are a million different situations when you have a choice: Be truthful and upset your loved one with Alzheimer's disease OR be kind and lie. The person with Alzheimer's disease cannot re-enter the "real world." You cannot convince her that her hallucinations are false or her remembrance of events is incorrect, so trying to "re-orient" her to reality is pointless. Furthermore, if you constantly correct her, she will grow less sure of herself, and perhaps depressed. To reiterate the principle set forth by Joanne Koenig Coste, the person with Alzheimer's will remember how you made her feel, even if she does not remember your exact words.[5] Choose kindness. Validate who she is, even in her confused state. In most cases, being right doesn't matter anymore.

---

[5] Learning To Speak Alzheimer's, Joanne Koenig Coste, Houghton – Mifflin, 2003, p. 50

Chapter 25

REALISTIC EXPECTATIONS

First, there are the excuses and rationalizations, the reasoning away of the increasingly frequent memory issues. "He's had surgery and is still confused from the anesthesia." "She's just getting older." "I'm not surprised she got lost. With all the road construction, the route to our house doesn't look the same anymore." Usually, there is some type of event that brings the family to reality. With Lester Potts, it was being fired from his "retirement job" of valet parking cars at the local hospital. Unknown to us, he would lose cars, lose keys, stay gone for over an hour to park a car, etc. Then, his doctor confirmed the diagnosis we were by that time expecting: Alzheimer's disease.

At this point in the process, every family wants to know what to expect. However, there are difficulties predicting the disease course in an individual, because it is different in every person. The disease process for Ellen's grandparents was very different from that of Daniel's father. Forming realistic expectations of what your loved one with Alzheimer's disease will go through, how long she will live, what difficulties she will have, is at best a moving target. There are some common themes, though, that you can reasonably expect over the rest of your loved one's life. We address many of the individual issues elsewhere in this book.

Length of illness: On average, a person lives another 7 to 10 years once he has been diagnosed with Alzheimer's disease. You can reasonably expect to add to or subtract from that number based on your loved one's general health and age when he gets the disease.

Search for Home: Most people with Alzheimer's disease are constantly searching for that which is familiar, and the most familiar place is home. Usually, this is the home in which she grew up, and not the home in which she lives now. Because of this, someone with Alzheimer's disease may go to the mailbox and wander away on the return to the house. It does not look like "home" to her. Note that even if the person is living in the home in which she grew up and always has lived, it can still look unfamiliar.

False Accusations: People with Alzheimer's disease often falsely accuse people of things, sometimes bizarre things. The most common of these accusations is stealing. These accusations are commonly directed at the caregiver, but often at others, too. These "others" can be either real or imaginary people. Daniel's Aunt Lola was certain that "a man in a strange suit" had stolen her potatoes, baked them, and returned them to her.

Hallucinations and altered perceptions are common and can take many forms. Your loved one may see herself in the mirror and believe it is someone else. She may believe people come to her house for evil purposes. Ellen's Grandmother Woodward lived in a dementia assisted living unit where the staff checked on the residents every two hours in the night. Mrs. Woodward once hit a staff member with a bed slat, because she thought the person was a burglar coming into her home. Daniel's grandmother believed the photograph of a baby given to her was a real child which she was responsible for feeding. She worried about the "baby" to the point that the family had to remove it. These altered perceptions also can have no basis in reality.

Memory Impairment: You can expect your loved one to grow increasingly forgetful. At first, the forgetfulness mainly takes the form of *forgetting names and where the person has put things.* Next, people begin *forgetting common tasks* (taking medication, brushing teeth, changing clothes, paying bills twice or not at all, etc.). People then begin *forgetting things that happened* (conversations, events, what she had for breakfast, etc.) As time goes on, your loved one will *forget how to do normal daily living tasks* (dressing, bathing, eating, etc.), and finally, will need these to be done for her. In the end stages of the disease, the person is usually bed-bound or wheelchair bound and may lose much of her ability to speak. Remember that even in the late stages the person is still there. She may respond to touch, familiar music, familiar stories, and other human interaction. The emotional self may remain somewhat intact. Keep trying to engage your loved one.

Dangers: If your loved one can walk, you can expect wandering and need to take precautions against it. Every person with Alzheimer's disease who can walk should have a GPS bracelet like those from Project Lifesaver (www.projectlifesaver.org). They prevent unnecessary tragedies. The person does not need to drive or operate machinery (lawn equipment, blenders and other cooking equipment, etc.) You can expect that things like kitchen knives, hedge clippers, lawnmowers, and other common household items will become dangerous in your loved one's hands. Secure these items, and especially, remove all firearms and incendiary devices from your home.

Sleep Disturbances: People with Alzheimer's disease often have difficulty sleeping through the night. When combined with the tendency to wander, this can be especially difficult to manage. As the caregiver, you need to make certain you get a good night's sleep whenever possible. Implement the suggestions given elsewhere in this book (see **SLEEPLESSNESS**).

Repeating Stories or Phrases: As your loved one loses more of his memories of the past, he will repeat a few stories (and later phrases) over and over again. He also may be fixated on an object associated with the story. For instance, Ellen's grandfather told a story about his great uncle who gave him a pistol. Then, he would retrieve the pistol (thankfully, unloaded!) and show anyone who would listen. Daniel's father would tell people, "I'm strong!" and flex his muscles for them. To strangers this looked very threatening.

Lack of Recognition: As time goes on, your loved one will lose the ability to recognize friends, then family members and other loved ones. He may call his wife's name, but not recognize her. For some, this happens in the middle stage, but for others, this does not happen until the late stage. Alzheimer's disease affects different people in different ways.

Less common issues which also occur are combativeness; verbal or physical abusiveness in people who have never had this issue before; loss of language relatively early in the disease process; loss of ability to read, write and / or spell relatively early in the disease process; improper and embarrassing public behavior (yelling, sexual behavior, talking to strangers as if they are friends, disrobing, etc.); seizures; and personality changes.

End Stage Alzheimer's Disease: Currently, Alzheimer's disease is a terminal illness. Many of those who have it die of other causes and never reach the end stage of the disease. For those who do, the caregiver can expect the person to lose the ability to walk and later, to sit up, to eat unassisted, and to communicate verbally. The person completely withdraws from her surroundings, but may still be able to interact through significant effort on the caregiver's part and through other modalities like touch or music. The affected person may still retain the ability to respond to touch, to interpret a smile, to be calmed from a gentle, soothing voice, etc. Ellen's grandmother was in this stage at her death. Her limbs were drawn inward to a fetal position and they could not be extended. She had to be turned every two hours to prevent painful bedsores.

There is no moral and ethical way to sugar-coat the realities of Alzheimer's disease. However, our hope is that families who are prepared for the realities of the disease will be better able to deal with them.

Chapter 26

SOCIAL ISOLATION

Caring for a loved one with Alzheimer's disease can be one of the most socially isolating occupations on the planet. Let's face it: visiting someone with Alzheimer's disease can be awkward. Most people avoid it. They don't know what to say. Sometimes the person with Alzheimer's disease does or says things that are socially unacceptable. The caregiver often is uncomfortable, worried about how their loved one will act or what he will say. For some people, visiting a loved one with Alzheimer's disease is too painful a task. Friends and family alike stop visiting, and the caregiver stops taking her loved one places for fear of wandering or how he will behave.

By the same process, the caregiver can leave home less and less, because her loved one requires higher levels of care, and it is not safe for him to stay at home by himself. As the disease progresses, your loved one may only want you, only remember you, and become agitated when you are gone. Sitters who will stay with those with Alzheimer's disease are difficult to find and expensive. As time goes on, it may become more trouble than it is worth to leave him, or the cost may be prohibitive.

Fewer visitors + decreased ability to leave the home = Social Isolation

Just when you need a social support network the most, you have the least access to it.

This situation is difficult to avoid for any caregiver, but especially for an Alzheimer's caregiver, because you cannot reason with someone who has Alzheimer's disease. You cannot tell him you will be home in a few hours, that you need to get out of the house for a little while or take a vacation. You cannot tell him not to say or do inappropriate things in public or in front of visitors.

In other parts of this book, we cover respite care options like adult daycare, scheduling family members to take turns sitting with your loved one, and residential facilities which may offer respite care if they have beds available (See **CARE / LIVING ARRANGEMENTS**). However, if you are at home with your loved one in an area that has no respite care available and you have no friends or relatives who are willing or able to help, here are some things you can do to keep social isolation at bay.

For many older people, computers are a way of keeping in touch with old friends and making new ones. Some companies even offer technology that can allow you to use the internet, receive e-mail, etc. on your television. Senior centers, community colleges, and faith-based organizations often offer free or low-cost computer classes for older adults. Check with your local senior agency for options in your area.

Social media sites like Facebook connect people with long-lost friends. We have re-connected with people from childhood, now living around the world. Ask your friends. Many more of them than you would think use Facebook and other similar sites to keep up with friends and loved ones. Often, it starts as a way of keeping up with children and grandchildren, but ends up as a social outlet unimaginable a few years ago. One senior, who worked as a children's librarian for many years, now follows the children she knew via Facebook. Furthermore, there is some evidence to show that Facebook actually helps stave off memory loss in the elderly http://www.allfacebook.com/facebook-helps-stave-off-memory-loss-in-elderly-2011-04.

Additionally, there are numerous websites on the internet which allow caregivers to connect and share knowledge with each other. The sympathy of a person in like circumstances can be a Godsend. You may find yourself offering the benefit of your experience to others. We give a list of references (including many websites) at the end of this book.

Last, but not least, there is the old-fashioned telephone. Perhaps you could schedule specific times to call friends just to talk. If you belong to a faith community, talk to your pastor, rabbi, or other leaders about how the community can help you. It may be there are others in the congregation who are in like circumstances, and a new area of service is needed.

For caregivers more so than the rest of us, maintaining social ties takes effort, sometimes more than you may feel you have to give to the task. You need people to whom you can turn for help, even if only when you need a shoulder (literally or figuratively) to cry on. At the risk of being repetitive, caregiving is a marathon, not a sprint. You need not run this race alone.

Chapter 27

LIVING ARRANGEMENTS

Respite Care

There usually comes a time, either temporarily or permanently, when a caregiver needs respite. There is no shame in this and there should be no guilt. Respite care allows caregivers to "refuel," so they can continue to care for their loved ones effectively. The goal is to find a balance between what is good for your loved one with Alzheimer's disease and what is good for you as the caregiver. That matters. Often, caregivers of those with Alzheimer's disease die first. Don't contribute to that statistic. Caregiving is a marathon, not a sprint, so pace yourself. There are often options available for respite care. Utilize them so that you can continue to give your loved one the best possible care.

There is no law that says you have to bear the burden alone. Often, *family members* want to help. Let them. Give yourself some time off. When possible, it is better for the substitute family caregiver to come to your home, rather than taking your loved one with Alzheimer's out of his familiar environment into another. However, this may not be possible.

Good, trained sitters are difficult to find, but completely invaluable when you find them. To begin your search, ask friends who may have had similar needs. Often, they can recommend someone. There are bonded sitter services available, but the quality of the sitters is very inconsistent and the sitters may not receive any training specific to caring for someone with Alzheimer's. If you belong to a faith community, ask the minister, rabbi or other leader for a recommendation. There may be someone in the congregation who would be suitable. Sometimes, Alzheimer's disease assisted living units or nursing homes will have employees who are willing to work for a few hours at a time as sitters. Your local Alzheimer's support organization also can serve as a resource for this type care. When you find a sitter, have her stay first with your loved one while you are in the home. That way, you can monitor how she interacts with your loved one before your leave her alone. If you hire a sitter, make certain the agency performs a background check or find out through local law enforcement how you can order a criminal background check on the person. This is extremely important. You are asking the sitter to take care of a precious person.

Alzheimer's disease assisted living units, nursing homes and hospice units will sometimes offer respite care for few days to weeks if they have extra space. Check with the local Senior Center, Alzheimer's support organization or with your physician for respite care resources in your area.

Adult Daycare is a wonderful option when it's done well and when it's available! Evaluate any daycare center before leaving your loved one there. What is a day like there? Do they offer art and music therapy? How much is the TV utilized? In the best daycare centers, the television is utilized very little or not at all. Spend some time in the center. Is it fun? How do the employees treat the clients? You are looking for a happy, cheerful, affirming and cognitively stimulating environment for your loved one. Alzheimer's disease daycare can be an incredible help to caregivers, especially those who need / want to stay in the workforce while caring for their loved one at home. Some states offer vouchers or grants to help pay for the cost of care. Check with the local Alzheimer's support organization or senior service agency.

Home healthcare is certainly a help, but in general, their employees do not provide respite care. Home health personnel come for specific tasks --- bathing, medical checks, blood draws, etc. They are not sitters and stay in your home only a short time. Do not substitute home healthcare for real respite care, and do not let family members tell you respite care is unnecessary because home health personnel visit your loved one.

Being a caregiver is one of the most stressful situations in the world. If you want to survive caregiving, allow yourself respite time. No one can be Superman or Wonder Woman. Please take care of yourself.

Should you consider residential care?

No one wants to place his loved one in a facility, but sometimes it is unavoidable. Whatever your reasons for considering this option, they are valid. Each caregiver has different gifts, limitations and circumstances. Each person with Alzheimer's disease has different behavioral and medical issues. Do not ever let anyone guilt you into keeping your loved one at home when you are nearing the limit of what you can do.

How often have you heard one of the following: "Mom said never to put her in a nursing home," or "You will NEVER put MY father in a nursing home!" or "I should be able to do this! My friend kept her husband at home for years!" If you are the primary caregiver, none of these types of statements should enter into your decision.

Try to evaluate your situation objectively. This is difficult, sometimes impossible, to do and is affected by myriad factors. If you cannot separate the emotional issues from the fact-based issues, you need help. Discuss your situation with a trusted family member, friend, rabbi, minister, counselor or physician. If you are so isolated that you can think of no objective person with whom to discuss this decision, the answer is clear: You need help with your loved one, whatever form that takes.

Ask yourself these questions: Does your loved one allow you to sleep at night? Does he wander away from your home or do you fear he will wander away? Have you put off doing things for your own personal health (doctor's visits, surgeries, diagnostic procedures, dental work, etc.), because caregiving does not allow you time for this? Is your loved one ever violent or physically hard to handle? Does she need more help than you can provide in activities of daily living (eating, dressing, bathing, toileting, lifting, etc.)? Does your loved one have dangerous habits at home (cooking, trying to drive the car, smoking, lighting fires, etc.)?

There may be other questions to ask, but these are a good start. The more questions to which you answered "yes," the more you need to seriously consider placing your loved one in a facility or getting some type of help at home.

Choosing a Residential Facility

Between the two authors of this book, we have had family members in 15 different dementia care facilities, ranging from daycare to nursing home care and everything in between. The quality of the facilities varied from atrocious to excellent. Many facilities that purport to be "specialty dementia units" are nothing more than locked nursing homes floors. You want to feel good about the quality of care where you place your loved one.

First, you need to understand there are several types of residential facilities. The first is "independent living," which is little more than an apartment in an eldercare community. This type living arrangement would be inappropriate for a person with Alzheimer's unless she is in the earliest stage. Next, there is "assisted living," where the resident lives in her own apartment, but receives assistance with daily living tasks --- medication, bathing, dressing, etc. This category is divided into "memory care" assisted living (for those with Alzheimer's and other memory issues) and regular assisted living for those people who are mentally capable, but need help physically. The "memory care" units are locked facilities which offer precautions against wandering. The third type of residential facility is the nursing home or healthcare facility, which may or may not be a locked unit. It is generally suitable for those who are nearing end stage or are in end stage Alzheimer's disease.

In general, independent living facilities are entirely paid by the individual or her family. Assisted living facilities are either paid by the individual / family or by long term care insurance, which usually does not cover the entire cost of care. Nursing home care can be covered by the individual / family, long term care insurance, Medicare (in some cases) or Medicaid (in some cases).

For any nursing home facilities which accept Medicare (and most do) a state survey is required to rate the quality of care in the facility. This is similar to a health department grading of a restaurant with specific criteria and scores / deductions given for specific infractions. The general results are available online free of charge. The complete survey is available for a fee online or to view free of charge at the nursing home, which must allow you to see a copy of its state survey upon request. In the survey, look at the CNA (Certified Nursing Assistant) staff retention rate (>80% is best), the number of bedsores in the facility, and weight loss statistics. Watch the residents. Do most of them seem drugged? Watch their mouths. If lots of the patients seem to be continually sticking out their tongues or if they look like they are chewing, this is a sign that they are being given anti-psychotic medications. Sometimes these are necessary, but not in the majority of patients. The things mentioned above are suggestions from former nursing home administrators.

Here are other factors to consider:

1. *Cleanliness:* Is the facility clean? Is there an unpleasant smell throughout? (Note that incontinent patients are usually changed just

before shift change, so the smell in any facility will be worse then.)

2. *Staff:* Spend some time in the facility and watch the staff. Are they interacting with the patients or sitting behind a desk? Are they kind? Do they treat the residents with respect?
3. *Administration:* Are resident populations with differing needs mixed? (i.e. Regular nursing home residents, those with Alzheimer's / dementia, and psychiatric inpatients should be kept separate.)
4. Does the *decor* aid those with Alzheimer's disease in overcoming their perception problems?
   a. Few patterns
   b. No mirrors
   c. No shiny floor or multi-colored, patterned carpet
   d. Darker, contrasting colored walls behind toilet and sink
   e. Plates in a medium tone that would contrast from the color of the food
5. What are the activities? Are art and music therapy offered? Who performs this therapy? Ideally, music and art therapy should be performed by licensed therapists in these fields, but sometimes that is not possible. If high quality music and art activities are offered by trained staff or volunteers, this is an acceptable substitute. Artist's supplies, not children's coloring books, crayons, etc., should be used for art activities. Music activities should be an interactive process with a live musician. One facility said they offered music therapy, but in reality, what they did was play a karaoke DVD on the television. This certainly does not qualify as music therapy.

6. What training is given to the staff before their first day on the job? What continuing education is offered to and required of the staff? All nurses have to have continuing education to keep their licenses, but it does not have to be job specific. Often, nurses enroll in whatever courses meet the requirements for the number of hours they need at the time they can attend, without consideration for the subject matter. Worse yet, aides often receive NO continuing education, and sometimes no real training prior to beginning their jobs.
7. Is there a secure courtyard or area where people can enjoy the outdoors in good weather?
8. Is there enough seating for everyone in the common area? In one 20 bed dementia assisted living facility, the common area seating consisted of a regular sized couch and two wing chairs. They had no activities and nothing to do but watch TV. At most, there was room for 6 people in front of the television. Everyone else had to sit in dining room chairs across the room.

Most of all, trust the feeling you get from the facility. If you have a bad feeling about the place, do not trust them with your loved one.

Parents Moving into their Children's Homes

As our population ages, more adult children are faced with decisions about where their parents should live if they are no longer able to live by themselves. It may be that the parent does not yet need nursing home care, which might be covered by Medicaid, but has no money for assisted living. It may be that the child wants to care for her parent at home. Whatever the reason, if you are considering this, you need to look at the situation from all sides, count the cost objectively, and then make your decision. In some cases, the decision may be forced upon you. If you have a choice about moving your parent into your home, you need to consider the changes this will make in your life.

If your parent cannot stay at home by himself, will there be enough money to pay for sitters or daycare? If not, will other family members be able to take shifts staying with him? If this is the case, all family members need to understand how their lives will change and willingly accept the task at hand. Caregiving for a parent in the home can be particularly hard on a marriage, especially if one spouse is not in full agreement about the living arrangements. If the adult child typically gives preference to the parent's wishes over the spouse's, marital problems usually follow. If you, your spouse or your children do not get along well with your parent, the situation will likely deteriorate when your parent moves into your home. If any of these family issues sound like your family, you should investigate other options. If there is no choice about your parent moving into the home, you should investigate periodic family and marriage counseling.

You also need to consider the level of care your parent needs, both now and as the disease progresses, and plan as much as is possible for the changes that will come. These may have long-term financial ramifications for your family if you or your spouse must quit work or work part-time to care for your parent. Your loved one may be able to stay by himself now, but chances are that will change. Will you or your spouse be able to afford to stay at home full time with him?

The presence of a grandparent with Alzheimer's disease in the home affects children's lives significantly. As your parent requires a higher level of care, the children's lives outside of home and school may be curtailed or outside activities may be cut completely. Lydia, whose grandmother lived in her home when she was growing up, said her mother never came to any of her school functions or anything else, because her mother was at home caring for her grandmother. Additionally, Lydia could never go anywhere unless a friend could provide all transportation, because her mother was at home with her grandmother. Years have passed and Lydia's mother is nearing a time when she may need to move out of her own home into more supervised care. She expects to move into Lydia's home, but Lydia is not willing to provide that level of care. Looking at the situation realistically, Lydia wants to be more active in her children's lives than she could be if she was caring for her mother. Also, Lydia knows that she and her husband do not get along well with her mother. Lydia has made the best decision for her family, even though her mother would disagree.

All these questions may sound selfish, but they are realities that should be considered. When both spouses are not fully invested in caregiving, it can cause friction, and increase distance and resentment as one spouse is engulfed by the sheer enormity of the caregiving task. This also holds true with the children.

Before your parent moves into your home, have a family meeting where you discuss all the issues we have mentioned and others you may have. If your parent is mentally able to participate, involve him/her.

1. Set parameters, boundaries and rules in writing. It is much easier to set the rules in advance, than to deal with the hurt feelings and other ramifications later!
2. If you are married, set a standing date night with your spouse at least once a month. Make sure your relationship and your marriage is not sacrificed to the task of caregiving.
3. If you have children, make time for each child every day.
4. Involve the entire family in specific caregiver tasks. Set a schedule so each family member knows what his / her duties are.
5. If possible, schedule vacation time away from your parent while he stays with another family member, a paid caregiver, or in an residential facility which offers respite care. Caregiving is a 24/7 job. The entire family will need time off.
6. If you have siblings, consider a shared arrangement for caregiving. In one family, the mother with Alzheimer's disease lives with each of her three children for the same four months every year. Everyone takes a turn. Everyone gets a break. Everyone knows what's expected. The only issue would be the transition time from home to home for the first week or two the parent is staying with each child.
7. ***Keep the humor in caregiving***! Laughter will keep your entire family sane. It is the

best defense we have against the darkness of Alzheimer's disease.

We have seen families in caregiving situations where a family member finds out what the expectations are ONLY when she fails to meet them, and the expectations are a moving target anyway. Delineating them (preferably in writing) is a way to prevent this from happening, insomuch as it is possible.

There is one more very disturbing family dynamic which bears mention. There are people whose personalities are not suited to caregiving, but who are caring for a family member in their home. Consider this scenario: An aging father comes to live with adult daughter and son-in-law. The daughter and son-in-law are resentful of the care they provide, and treat the father as a stupid, worthless burden. They criticize the father, his actions, and his lack of abilities all the time. As they do this, their children observe this behavior and do likewise. The children are learning how to treat elderly people, and how to treat their own parents as they grow older. If you think this could describe the way you might treat your loved one, or if you are in this situation now, do your best to change the family dynamic or investigate other care options.

Chapter 28

SECONDARY CAREGIVERS

Secondary caregivers are those individuals, usually family members, who do not have primary responsibility for the person with Alzheimer's, but may help from time to time, or may have an interest in the person's care. These would include children, grandchildren, siblings, even parents of the person with Alzheimer's disease.

Your role should be that of helpful supporter, giving your time, a listening ear, a shoulder to cry on, or any other support within your power to give. In general, don't criticize. Most primary caregivers do the best they can under extremely difficult circumstances. They develop coping mechanisms and routines that work for them. Barring some type of crisis (abuse, dangerous practices, etc.), you should not try to change these.

Never make guilt-producing statements to the primary caregiver, such as "You promised you would never put Dad in a nursing home!" Unless you are willing to take full responsibility for your loved one's care, you should not try to keep the primary caregiver from making decisions she feels are best for your loved one, like getting sitters, enrolling him in dementia daycare, moving him to a residential facility, etc. There is enough guilt involved in these decisions without secondary caregivers adding to it. However, if you feel the primary caregiver is "burning out," becoming depressed, or if you have other concerns, definitely talk about these with the primary caregiver and make recommendations about respite care or other alternatives.

There is one exception to this rule. If you feel the primary caregiver is physically or emotionally abusing the person, you need to take prompt action to protect the person with Alzheimer's disease, up to and including calling law enforcement, if the primary caregiver cannot be convinced to place her loved one in a facility or in another's care immediately. More often, the abuse is verbal and not physical. If this is the case, try to gently redirect the primary caregiver. Give her this book or others that advocate for kindness and respect in the treatment of those with Alzheimer's disease. If this does not work, you may need to talk with her about your concerns. Often, the verbal (or even physical) abuse is fueled by the incredible stress under which the primary caregiver lives every day. This may lead to a helpful discussion of issues of respite care or residential care that have been weighing on her mind.

Support the primary caregiver. Love the person with Alzheimer's. These are your words to live by.

Chapter 29

THE PHYSICIAN, the PATIENT, and the CAREGIVER

The physician - patient relationship is among the most sacred in the world, but when the patient has Alzheimer's disease, that relationship becomes more complicated for everyone. The most important thing in choosing a physician for your loved one with Alzheimer's disease is to find someone who partners with you, understands the disease process and difficulties of Alzheimer's disease, and understands the responsibilities of caregiving. That physician may be a neurologist, a geriatrician, a psychiatrist, an internist, or a family practitioner. However, as the caregiver, you need to know there are nuances to managing Alzheimer's disease patients that doctors who do not care for them regularly would not know. Also, you must understand there are responsibilities on both sides of the doctor - patient / caregiver relationship.

First, medicine is an art, not a cookbook, and that is nowhere more true than in managing the care of someone with Alzheimer's disease. Expect that some things the physician tries will not be effective, or may have negative side effects, for your loved one. Be willing to work with the physician. If your loved one's behavior or condition worsens after changing medications, notify the physician immediately. Don't wait for the next visit. Note that pharmaceutical company ads are designed to sell drugs, not to prescribe them. Trust your physician's recommendations, not the ads you see on TV.

Your loved one's physician should be a good resource for coordinated care --- home health, daycare, hospice, assisted living, nursing home, etc. He also should be a neutral third party who views things more objectively than either the caregiver or the person with Alzheimer's. Follow the physician's medical recommendations to the letter and consider seriously (and objectively, if possible) recommendations regarding care, such as placing your loved one in a residential facility, placing him on hospice care, enrolling him in Alzheimer's daycare, etc. Most caregivers have not been through this process before, but an experienced physician has. Trust his recommendations.

In the patient's presence, many caregivers do not feel comfortable telling the physician about behavioral and other issues their loved ones have. If this is the case, a few days before the doctor visit, send the physician a letter or e-mail detailing your concerns in as few words as possible while still covering the subject. The doctor can address these issues in the examination room without it seeming that you have alerted him to the issues. When the doctor is talking to your loved one and asking questions, do not interrupt! It is very important that your loved one be allowed to express himself in his own way and at his own speed without someone else attempting to answer. Listening to the patient is another way by which the physician evaluates him. Though well-intentioned, this effort to answer for the person can be frustrating for the patient, and actually can cause him to lose his train of thought. It is validating to the person with Alzheimer's disease to be able to speak for himself.

If you need to add information after your loved one has spoken, you will have the opportunity to do so.

NEVER send a person with Alzheimer's disease to the doctor without accompanying him! There is no substitute for a responsible caregiver as an advocate for her loved one. Often, a person with Alzheimer's disease living in a residential facility is transported by ambulance to a physician's office with no caregiver in attendance. If the person does not have the ability to answer for himself or to remember the physician's recommendations, the visit is a waste of time. As the caregiver, it is your responsibility to be able to answer for your loved one *if he cannot answer coherently for himself*, to watch after your loved one's interests, and to implement the doctor's orders. When you go to the doctor, always take a list of the person's medications and their exact dosage schedule with you to the visit.

Nearly all those with Alzheimer's have behavioral issues at one time or another. If certain behaviors are a particular problem, keep a log of them and present it to the physician at his next visit. Write down questions before the doctor visit, so you will not need to call afterward.

If your loved one's condition changes markedly or suddenly, have him evaluated by his physician. This can indicate infection, stroke, or other serious problems.

Finally, your pharmacist is a valuable partner in patient care. Use the same pharmacy for all your loved one's medications, so the pharmacist has a complete list and can watch for drug interactions. If there is a potential for a drug interaction, the pharmacist may recognize it when the physician does not, especially if multiple physicians prescribe medication for your loved one.

Chapter 30

DEALING WITH DIFFICULT FAMILY MEMBERS

Picture this: A loving wife cares for her husband with Alzheimer's disease, day in, day out. She partners with her physician, feels comfortable with him, and together they have developed an excellent plan to deal with her husband's condition. Her son comes for visits only to criticize the care his mother gives, his father's condition, the poor medical care that contributes to it, the food fed to his father, the fact that the house should be cleaner, his mother's worry that she may have to place his father in a facility, etc. You name it, family members have probably criticized it.

The first thing you should do is to realize that most criticism arises from shock, grief, guilt, and feelings of helplessness. The caregiver sees her loved one every day. From her point of view, his decline is very gradual, almost imperceptible. To the son, it seems as if his father has fallen off an Alzheimer's cliff. Talking on the phone to someone is not the same as seeing him try to accomplish tasks. Also, caregivers often do not paint a realistic picture of the situation in the home. "How are things, Mom?" "Fine, dear."

That being said, you need family support, not criticism. The best way for your family members to gain understanding is to experience what you experience. Ellen's grandmother and mother used to leave Ellen to care for her grandfather when their family would come for visits. In this way, she understood to a small extent what her grandmother's life as a caregiver was like. In our scenario, the mother should leave the son to care for his father while she gets some much-needed respite.

Another way to deal with criticism is to take it as an offer of help. Your daughter criticizes how dirty the house is? Respond with, "It really does need cleaning! Would you rather clean the house or watch your father while I clean?"

Unfortunately, sometimes you have to confront criticism head-on. Strive for a firm and loving tone. Talk honestly about the issues you face, especially the really serious ones --- living arrangements, finances, your need for respite, etc. Often, this will resolve the situation. If it does not and the family member still is critical, respond with this, "Please do not criticize me unless you are willing to take over your father's care." Try not to escalate the discussion into an argument if possible. It takes two to argue. Refuse to become the second person in the argument.

The journey through Alzheimer's disease is difficult for everyone and each person deals with it in his own way. Some lash out, others withdraw, some grieve publicly, some privately. Stand firm, but do so gracefully.

Chapter 31

MUSIC, ART, AND ALZHEIMER'S DISEASE

The brain is a mysterious organ! One would think that singing and speaking would be located in the same general area, that an inability to speak also would indicate an inability to sing. Such is not the case. Lester Potts had not spoken in several months when he went to an inpatient hospice unit. However, when we would sing the hymns of his childhood, he could join in singing them. If you can find the songs that are most familiar --- religious songs if the person is religious (or was religious in childhood) and / or songs from the person's teens and early 20's --- these can often "awaken" those whom nothing else seems to reach.

There is a wonderful video on YouTube at http://www.youtube.com/watch?v=CrZXz10FcVM where Naomi Feil interacts with Gladys Wilson, a lady with late stage Alzheimer's disease. Mrs. Wilson is every person with late stage Alzheimer's we have passed in the halls of nursing homes everywhere, and thought these people were beyond human interaction, beyond help. The interaction between Feil and Wilson is amazing and humbling. Mrs. Wilson is still there. Naomi Feil is able to reach her through the music Mrs. Wilson sang all her life, in this case the religious songs of childhood.

There is a growing body of scientific research to support what many have observed for years in the reactions of those with Alzheimer's to music therapy. Dr. Carol A. Prickett is a Professor of Music Therapy and Music Education at the

University of Alabama. In Geriatric Neurology, a textbook to be published in late 2011 by Prentice - Hall, she asserts that people diagnosed with Alzheimer's disease and related dementias can continue participating in structured music activities late into the disease process, even playing instruments and participating in dance and movement. Social and emotional skills, including interaction and communication, can be improved during music sessions and for a period of time after the sessions conclude. Additionally, recall may be enhanced, particularly for personal memories, when music associated with those memories is sung or played. Music interventions can offer an excellent alternative to pharmaceutical or physical restraints in controlling agitation or wandering, or reduce the need for drugs and restraints. If you are evaluating music or music therapy offered in a facility, note that individual and small group settings are much better than large groups, where the therapist cannot give individual attention to the participants. Certainly, the music in therapy sessions needs to be provided by a live person, rather than by a CD or DVD. The others may be valuable tools at other times, but cannot be called music therapy.

If you do not have access to a board certified music therapist, your loved one still can receive some of the benefits of music. Play music from her teens and twenties. Sing it together. If the person has never played an instrument before, get her a tambourine or some maracas to use as rhythm instruments. Often, if someone played an instrument well before the onset of Alzheimer's disease, that person will retain the ability to play it well into the middle stages of the disease. This was the case with Daniel's grandmother, who was a church organist / pianist. She lost her ability to read music and learn new pieces, but could still play pieces she had memorized in earlier years on the piano. She was born in 1898, so the music she remembered from her heyday was Ragtime. After she developed dementia, the two styles would merge, and we would be entertained with "What a Friend We Have in Jesus" in the style of Scott Joplin. There have even been cases where the person with dementia became a better musician for a time after the diagnosis.

Those with Alzheimer's disease can benefit greatly from art and art therapy. Even if your loved one never exhibited artistic talent before his diagnosis with Alzheimer's disease, he may have hidden talent as an artist. Such was the case with Lester Potts, who became a watercolor artist at a point when he could no longer hammer a nail or change a light bulb. Because he had no access to a board certified art therapist, Lester was taught by a retired commercial artist who volunteered his time at Caring Days, the dementia daycare center Lester attended.

Similar to music therapy, studies show participants in art therapy to be more alert, more aware of their environment, more socially interactive, and have improved mood. Perhaps most importantly, it gives people who have difficulty with their verbal abilities, or who have lost the ability to speak altogether, a means of expression. Also, it gives them something to be proud of and the ability to express frustrations and feelings on paper, rather than with negative behaviors. The desired outcome is not a beautiful product, but self-expression of the artist.

In our own experience, Lester Potts, who was depressed before beginning art at Caring Days, began to smile again and was bursting with pride at his artistic creations. You can use some of these techniques at home. Purchase artist's supplies (NOT coloring books and crayons which are suitable only for children). Encourage your loved one to paint what she sees in a picture, an outdoor scene or from a staged "still life." Often, caregivers find their loved ones can concentrate for much longer periods of time than usual when creating art.

Other forms of "art" --- literature, poetry, sculpture, dance, drama, storytelling, etc. --- can benefit those with Alzheimer's disease, too. Read familiar passages from great works, especially those perhaps memorized by the person in her youth. When reading scripture or something in translation, make certain to read the translation used by the person in her youth. If there is a dance or drama therapy program in your community, consider having your loved one participate. These activities are particularly effective when performed with a group, such as at a daycare center. Recent studies show that expressive art therapies of any kind (art, music, dance, drama, etc.) reduce the number of trips to the doctor the person requires!

Pictures of familiar scenes, art, literature, poetry, scripture, music, etc. --- all these are tools to help you access your loved one as his Alzheimer's disease progresses. If you employ these tools, your loved one will benefit, and you will find ways to connect with him that you never imagined possible.

Chapter 32

THE HOLIDAY VISIT (A CASE STUDY)

Kate e-mailed us Christmas Day about her mother-in-law, Lily, whom Kate has suspected for some time has memory issues. These became especially apparent when Kate, her husband, and the rest of the family visited Lily for Christmas. Here are some excerpts from Kate's e-mail:

My 81-year-old mother-in-law is losing it. She can't remember anything. For months, everyone was making excuses, but today when she couldn't figure out how to use her washing machine, everyone saw the issue. She admits she has a problem, but won't call to make a doctor's appointment. She has even developed her own language now with all the replacement words and bizarre pronunciations! My father-in-law is physically in bad shape, so he can't really help. My husband wants me to handle everything, as does one of his brothers, as I am very close to Lily. The other brother is in denial. Could this be normal cognitive decline? What should we do?

If this describes any part of your holiday travel this year, you are not alone. Often, a loved one's memory issues are revealed during holiday visits. Over the phone, those with Alzheimer's disease who live out of town can often cover their memory issues through something doctors call the "social facade." However, when they are faced with things that confuse their routine and make their lives more complicated --- a house full of company, large meals to cook, meat to grill, turkeys to carve, an unfamiliar environment, etc. --- memory problems are revealed in ways that even the most fervently denying family member must recognize.

Here is our advice for Kate and her family:

First of all, don't expect Lily to call and make her own appointment with her physician. Lily may not have the mental ability to do this. Some people with Alzheimer's disease lose their ability to read and write very early in the disease process. This was the case with Daniel's father. Even if Lily can read and write, looking up a phone number alphabetically and retaining that information long enough to dial the number is a very complicated process. Lily may not be able to do this.

In this case, Lily admits she has memory problems. However, admitting it and being brave enough to call the doctor for an appointment (which may result in a diagnosis of Alzheimer's disease) are two different things. At this point, since Kate's husband and one of his brothers agree that Kate should take charge, Kate (who is willing to do this) should call the doctor, make the appointment, and accompany Lily for the visit. If the primary care doctor is not very knowledgeable about Alzheimer's disease care, Kate should ask for a referral to a geriatrician, neurologist, or geriatric psychiatrist. Also, Kate could consider requesting a neuropsychology profile, which helps determine if depression plays any part in Lily's memory issues, in addition to helping confirm the diagnosis and stage. Lily is caregiver to an invalid husband, a difficult and sometimes depressing job, so the likelihood that depression plays a role is increased.

One more very important test which the physician could order is a driving evaluation by an occupational therapist. Lily may be a danger to herself and others when behind the wheel. If Lily's keys should be taken away, the physician should be the one to do it with the family in attendance.

Next, Kate should educate herself about Alzheimer's disease (see **RESOURCES**).

The family should discover what legal arrangements there are for Lily if she is impaired. Does she have a living will? Has she given someone power of attorney, healthcare power of attorney, etc.? Someone (or more than one person) needs to be delegated this power by Lily if she is still able to do it. Lily and her family should visit an elder law attorney in the state where Lily lives.

A spinal tap and other highly invasive procedures to confirm a diagnosis of Alzheimer's disease are not necessary. A good clinician can be greater than 95% sure she is dealing with Alzheimer's disease without a spinal tap. Given that the physician ruled out other causes for Lily's memory issues through examination, MRI, simple blood tests, and perhaps a neuropsychology profile, the treatment options will not change significantly even if Lily does not technically have Alzheimer's disease.

Be understanding with the brother who is in denial. Every family member of a person with Alzheimer's disease has been in denial at some point, the authors of this book included. Given Lily's condition, the brother will not be able to stay in denial too much longer. If Lily does receive an Alzheimer's diagnosis, Kate and her husband, armed with the results of the doctor's tests, will have to talk with her husband's brother. However, even if he has to admit Lily has Alzheimer's, he may always deny that the disease process is as advanced as it is. His perception of his mother's disease process always may be step-wise, as he is shocked into reality again and again, rather than the more gradual decline the other family members observe.

The family should begin talking to Lily now about alternative living arrangements where both Lily and her husband can get the care they need. The time is coming very soon when this will be necessary, and it is MUCH better to make these decisions (with the participation of the parties involved, if possible) before a crisis arises. The family, Lily, and her husband may want to consider choosing a facility now and placing Lily and her husband on the waiting list, if there is one. You don't want to begin your search for a facility in a crisis situation and be forced to move your loved one into anywhere that has availability.

Finally, the biggest trap of caregiving is guilt. Do your best not to fall into it. There is always guilt about not spending enough time caregiving, spending too much time caregiving and away from your own family, misleading Lily so that you can go get through the day without causing fights, telling Lily the truth and unwittingly starting an argument, etc. Kate needs to realistically determine how she can care for Lily, given that they live 5 hours apart. The siblings need to decide how they will split the care duties among themselves in a way that will be fair to everyone. Caregiving for someone with Alzheimer's disease is a difficult task.

Chapter 33

END OF LIFE CARE

No experience can be more heart-rending, or precious, than caring for a loved one at the end of his life. We have been through this personally with our own family members, as well as professionally with patients and their families. Although each Alzheimer's caregiver's experience with end of life care is different, perhaps we may provide some guidance that will be helpful.

Ideally, planning for end of life care should occur much earlier in life, when mental capacity is not in question. If your loved one has not done this, it should happen soon after the diagnosis of Alzheimer's disease is made, and when your loved one is still able to express his wishes. This should be documented with the assistance of an eldercare attorney in the forms of a living will, advanced healthcare directive, and healthcare proxy. This will take much of the stress and responsibility off you as the caregiver when these directives have to be carried out. Moreover, you will have the added assurance that you are following your loved one's wishes. If you have not done this planning for yourself, you should take the opportunity to do it at the same time. In the words of Ellen's grandmother, "It's always later than you think." Mental or physical disability can occur at any time during life.

As the disease advances, your loved one may loose the ability to speak, swallow, walk, and care at all for himself. If he survives to the last stages of the disease, he will be bed-bound, unable to speak, contracted in his arms and legs, and will require total care. Often, in this debilitated state, he will succumb eventually to infection, either from aspiration pneumonia, blood infection from skin breakdown, or urinary tract infection that gets into the bloodstream. Whether or not to aggressively treat these infections as they occur should have been addressed with prior planning. However, no amount of preparation makes it easy to withdraw care or decide not to use it in the first place. With the scientifically advanced state of our modern healthcare system, we can effectively treat and cure most infections. However, in the weakened, debilitated state of one with advanced Alzheimer's disease, cure is not possible. We would suggest that aggressive care for one in such a state qualifies as prolonging suffering rather than relieving it.

The sooner you accept the terminal state of your loved one, the more meaningful, peaceful, and compassionate will be his death experience. Many caregivers rely strongly on their spiritual lives and faith to get them through. We recommend you seek counseling or guidance from the clergy in your particular walk of faith to support you as you go. Additionally, friends and family members can reminisce with you about your loved one's life, and help you remember the time when Alzheimer's was not an issue. When you are in the throws of caregiving, this is sometimes difficult to do.

We strongly advocate for hospice care for anyone who has a terminal illness, but especially the person with Alzheimer's who is nearing the end of life. We cannot say enough good things about our experiences with hospice, both inpatient and outpatient. If you are not familiar with hospice care, you may be tempted to think of it as lack of care, withdrawal of care, or a dark, depressing place where your loved one is left to die. Nothing could be farther from the truth! Hospice professionals (including nurses, chaplains, social workers, music and art therapists, etc.) are specially trained to deliver the ultimate in compassionate, comforting care to the person with Alzheimer's disease and caregivers. The whole environment is one of peace and comfort. Hospice feels like home, perhaps the "home" your loved one has been looking for. Also, hospice benefits generally are covered by Medicare. If your loved one with Alzheimer's disease is nearing the end of life, ask the physician for a hospice referral to see if she may qualify.

In the last few weeks of his father's life, Daniel had the opportunity to meet with his dad and tell him everything he had ever wanted to say to him. This was a blessing and an honor, but it is not always possible. Even if this cannot be done, express your feelings openly with family and friends if you can. Focus on powerful, pleasant memories if feasible. This can help to bring closure.

Many people have "unfinished business" of the negative variety with the person who has Alzheimer's disease. There may be wrongs that have never been righted, relationships that were damaged, or any number of other occurrences which have caused difficulties along the way. Hospice counselors can help you deal with this unfinished business, whether or not your loved one can respond.

The issue of artificial nutrition was addressed earlier in this handbook. By the time you find yourself in this position, you already should have clear direction about what to do. We again emphasize that there is no right or wrong way to approach this issue. For some, the most humane decision is to withdraw all forms of nourishment and medications, except those that are providing comfort. For some, this is too difficult. Please seek the counsel and support of professionals as you make these decisions. We err on the side of not prolonging the dying experience, but you as the caregiver must follow your heart and the wishes of your loved one.

Witnessing the actual death of a loved one is an intense experience and is not for every caregiver. However, if it is your desire to be present, the actual timeframe may be somewhat more predictable if your loved one is under hospice care, because the person's condition is so closely monitored. Daniel and his mother were present with his father in Hospice of West Alabama at the moment of death, and it was an experience that was precious for them.

Caregivers often find themselves lost after the death of their loved ones, not only because of grief, but also because they have been so focused on caregiving that they have thought of little else for years. This is a natural phenomenon, and one that will fade with time. Again, it is recommended that grief counseling be considered as a means of healing for the caregiver. Hospice care provides this for families after a loved one's death. After your grief has time to heal somewhat, consider volunteering your time in areas of service in the community. This often will help to ease the pain and feelings of loss which are inevitable.

At the end of your journey you can look back and know you did the best job you could to care for your loved one and make each moment matter for them. This race is not for the faint of heart, but the running is easier for the well-prepared.

Chapter 34

LOVING THOSE WITH ALZHEIMER'S THE WAY THEY ARE

Often, the family caregiver, who sacrifices so much for her loved one with Alzheimer's disease, has the most difficult time loving the individual as he is, because her view is so clouded by grief over who the person once was and will never be again. This is by no means a criticism of caregivers. The love they show 24 hours a day, 7 days a week is a phenomenal testament to sacrificial love that has few parallels. The situation is complicated by the fact that the descent into Alzheimer's disease is a gradual process. In the beginning, you begin to notice that your loved one is repeating himself, getting some things wrong, confusing some things. Any logical person would correct him. As the process continues and your loved one is diagnosed with Alzheimer's disease, you strive to bring back the person you knew and loved as he once was.

The breakthrough comes when you realize he can't be brought back. When you learn that you must meet him in his "now," which may well not be your "now." In essence, you must grieve the loss of the one you loved, and learn to love anew. Each of us, no matter how infirm or debilitated, is still a human being with needs, hopes, and drives. All of us need to feel loved for being ourselves, to be accepted, and to be validated for who we are, even if that "who" is revealing itself for the first time with every passing day.

The person with Alzheimer's disease has entered a different realm, one in which people and things are less and less familiar, reality is askew, time has lost its meaning, and connection is no longer maintained with the world in which he lives. This is not a conscious decision made by your loved one with Alzheimer's. It is an unavoidable consequence of the disease process. Also, it serves to isolate your loved one in his own cocoon of confusion, frustrate the caregiver who can no longer "reach" the one she has known and loved, and further destroy the self-identity of the person suffering from Alzheimer's. Furthermore, as we lose contact with one whom we have loved, we lose contact with part of ourselves.

The key to coming to terms with this loss is to realize that the human being we have known and loved is still there, but his persona has been masked by Alzheimer's disease. We must strive to look deep within, past the speechless eyes and blank stare, to the heart. Though memory, orientation, language, and other cognitive elements are fading, the emotional self remains. Likewise, the ability to recall remote memories and experiences remains to some extent. It becomes the caregiver's task, then, to reach into the deepest parts of the self and try to connect. Every perceptive and communicative modality may be called upon in this task...touch, smell, sight, reminiscence, as well as the expressive arts (art, music, dance, poetry, drama, etc). Verbal expression can no longer be relied upon as the primary means of communication. We must give the person a full palette from which to paint. And if we earnestly observe and listen with all our skills, we may just learn the new "language" of our loved one: the language of the heart.

The outcome of this approach is validation, both for the one with Alzheimer's disease *and* the caregiver. For when we learn to love and accept them in their "now," we do the same for ourselves.

PART II

QUICK REFERENCE

ALZHEIMER'S DISEASE: THE BASICS

The 10 Warning Signs of Alzheimer's Disease[6]

1. Short term memory loss that disrupts daily life
2. Difficulties in planning or solving problems
3. Difficulty completing familiar tasks
4. Confusion with time or place
5. Trouble understanding what one sees
6. New problems with words in speaking or writing
7. Misplacing things and losing the ability to retrace steps
8. Decreased or poor judgment
9. Withdrawal from work or social activities
10. Changes in mood and personality

---

[6] http://www.alz.org/alzheimers_disease_10_signs_of_alzheimers.asp

The 4 "A's" of Alzheimer's Disease[7]

1. *Amnesia* - short term memory loss
2. *Aphasia* - language disturbance
3. *Apraxia* - inability to do learned tasks
4. *Agnosia* - inability to recognize familiar people or objects

The L's of Caregiving

1. *Live* in their world.
2. *Love* them as they are
3. *Learn* to value remaining talents / gifts
4. *Let* them maintain structured independence
5. *Listen, listen, listen*
6. *Laugh* with them
7. *Line up* respite opportunities
8. *Linger* over pleasant memories
9. *Look* past the "scribbling" to the "art"

---

[7] [7] http://www.alzbrain.org/pdf/handouts/2003.%20DEMENTIA.pdf

"We have a diagnosis, now what?"

1. Make sure your loved one understands she has a problem with her memory and cognitive function.

2. Seek the services of an eldercare attorney for will, living will, power of attorney, healthcare proxy, etc.

3. Develop a care plan incorporating "off" time for yourself.

4. Locate the nearest Alzheimer's caregiver support group and consider attending meetings.

5. Address driving safety.

6. Address family finances and management of accounts.

7. Ensure your loved one takes his medication correctly.

8. Begin using memory aids, such as calendars, lists, etc.

9. Establish a routine for your loved one.

10. Place information for important contacts in easy-to-find sites.

11. Make home modifications for safety and independence.

12. Investigate availability of well-trained dementia sitters.

13. Inform family and friends of your loved one's diagnosis and care plan.

14. Attend scheduled doctor visits with your loved one.

15. Keep an updated health history and list of medications for your loved one close at hand.

16. Learn to laugh with your loved one. Do not feel guilty about it!

17. Develop an attitude of hope.

18. Learn to love her in her "now."

ARGUING and CORRECTING

1. Expect a person with Alzheimer's to believe things and say things that are completely unreasonable and illogical. It is part of the disease process.

2. If possible, find a way to avoid arguing or correcting your loved one with Alzheimer's disease.

3. Before you correct, argue, or disagree with your loved one with Alzheimer's, ask yourself, "Does it really matter?" Usually the answer is "no."

4. Find something to agree with or make a neutral comment like, "I can see why that would bother you," or "My goodness!"

5. If your loved one believes someone long dead to be alive, do not correct him.

6. If your loved one believes something bizarre to be true, do not correct him.

7. Over time, your loved one increasingly may lose touch with reality. Try to enter his world, instead of trying to pull him back to yours.

BATHROOM ISSUES

1. Cover mirrors in the bathroom and bedroom.

2. Paint walls behind the sink and commode a contrasting color (i.e. a medium blue or green behind a white commode and sink).

3. If your loved one refuses to take a bath, brush her teeth, change her clothes, etc., break the task into smaller sections ("Let's unbutton your blouse. Now, let's take off your blouse. Can you help me get your arms out?").

4. Maintain respect for her personal privacy. Keep her clothed or covered until the last possible minute.

5. Always have everything ready BEFORE you begin the disrobing / bathing process.

6. NEVER leave a person with Alzheimer's disease unattended while bathing her.

7. Bathe your loved one at the best time of day for her. Be flexible.

8. Make certain there is a rug or non-skid floor covering outside the tub or shower to keep your loved one from slipping.

9. Install hand rails and use a rubber mat on the tub or shower floor and around the commode to minimize the danger of slipping.

10. Use a shower / tub seat.

11. Install a shower head with an extension.

12. Expect your loved one to have bladder control problems and later bowel control issues.

13. Bladder infections are very common in people with Alzheimer's. Learn to suspect urinary tract infections if your loved one suddenly worsens in any way.

14. Report any worsening of your loved one's condition to the doctor.

CAREGIVER GUILT

1. Value your gift. Caregiving is the most difficult, grueling job on earth. You are giving your loved one the gift of yourself. No one can ask more than that.

2. Guilt is completely normal for caregivers.

3. Excessive guilt can be a sign of caregiver depression. If it becomes a problem, consult your physician.

4. Do not compare yourself to other caregivers. The situations are never the same.

5. Do the best you can in a difficult situation and forgive yourself when you do not or cannot meet your own expectations, those of your family, or those of your loved one with Alzheimer's disease.

6. Although other family members can have input, those who are not participating in your loved one's care do not have the right to criticize your best efforts as a caregiver.

7. Caregiving is a marathon, not a sprint. To finish the race, you must take care of yourself.

8. Expect your loved one with Alzheimer's NOT to like it when you spend time away from him. However, time away is necessary for you to stay mentally, physically, spiritually, and emotionally healthy.

9. If you believe it is time to place your loved one in a facility, do not allow other family members to criticize you for your decision. Only you can decide what you can and cannot do as a caregiver. No one else has walked a mile in your shoes.

10. Do not make promises you may not be able to keep --- "I'll never put Mom in a nursing home," or "I promised Dad he could die at home," etc.

11. Realize that you may have to lie or "stretch the truth" on occasion to keep your loved one from getting upset. This is perfectly acceptable.

DEPRESSION

Warning Signs:

1. Anxiety (anxious expression, worrying)
2. Sadness (sad expression, sad voice, tearfulness, crying)
3. Lack of reaction to pleasant events (no smiling, laughing, enjoyment)
4. Irritability (easily annoyed, short tempered)
5. Agitation (restlessness, handwringing, hair pulling)
6. Multiple physical complaints / Hypochondria
7. Acute Loss of interest (disinterest in usual activities)
8. Change in Appetite (eating more or less than usual with accompanying weight loss or gain)
9. Lack of energy (fatigues easily, unable to sustain activities)
10. Sleeping more or less than is normal
11. Suicide (feels life is not worth living, has suicidal wishes, or makes suicide attempt)
12. Self-depreciation (self-blame, poor self-esteem, feelings of failure and worthlessness)
13. Pessimism (anticipation of the worst)

What to do:

1. Consult your physician.

2. Consult your physician immediately if you or your loved one has thoughts of suicide.

3. Engage in activities both of you always have enjoyed if possible.

4. Find new activities. Art and music therapy are excellent options if available. If not, art (using supplies suitable for adults) and music (choosing songs familiar from childhood) are good choices.

5. Do not watch frightening or depressing things on television. Twenty-four hour coverage of tragic events on the news is particularly detrimental.

6. Take your loved one to adult Alzheimer's disease daycare, if a high quality facility of this kind is available.

7. For caregivers, stay as socially active as possible.

8. Do not correct or argue with your loved one.

9. Remove objects with which your loved one may harm himself or others.

DRESSING ISSUES

1. Break each dressing task into the smaller tasks, especially if she says she doesn't want to change clothes or has already changed clothes.

2. If public disrobing is not an issue, make sure clothing is easily changed.

3. If she can easily raise her arms, choose loose-fitting pullover shirts.

4. If she cannot easily raise her arms, choose zippered shirts or button-up shirts.

5. Choose slip-on or Velcro-fastened shoes with non-skid soles, "wash and wear" hairstyles, and pants or skirts with elasticized waistbands.

6. Buy nothing that requires ironing or dry cleaning for everyday wear.

7. Place clothing choices on a surface with contrasting color to that of the clothes (light against dark or dark against light).

8. If arguments over clothing choice are an issue, choose several outfits and allow your loved one to choose from those options.

9. Allow your loved one to choose for herself and don't worry about what she wears, unless it is a special occasion (wedding, funeral, etc.)

10. See **INAPPROPRIATE PUBLIC BEHAVIOR** if your loved one disrobes in public.

DRIVING ISSUES

1. Drivers with Alzheimer's disease can be a danger to themselves and others.

2. Caregivers must take the lead in getting their loved ones off the road.

3. Get your loved one's physician involved early. If there is any question about current driving safety, or if you have difficulties getting your loved one to stop driving, request a driver's evaluation from a qualified occupational therapist, which gives objective results on one's driving abilities.

4. Have your loved one's vision examined.

5. If your loved one is obsessed with a particular car, hide the keys, disconnect the battery, give it to a grandchild, etc.

6. If your loved one forgets he is not supposed to drive, get a note from the doctor to show him.

7. From the passenger seat, some people with Alzheimer's disease try to "help" the caregiver drive. You may need to move him to the back seat.

8. If your loved one tries to exit a moving vehicle, place him in the back seat and use the rear door child safety locks (check the car's owner's manual to see if you have these). If your car does not have them, you may need to discontinue taking your loved one places in the car.

EATING TOO LITTLE

1. Appetite (or lack of it) is controlled by the brain. If the part of the brain that tells your loved one he is hungry is affected, he may not want to eat.

2. Talk to your loved one's physician or a registered dietician.

3. Try to make sure everything your loved one eats is packed with nutrition.

4. Keep healthy snacks around the house, like cut fruit and vegetables.

5. Offer nutritious food often.

6. Make certain the color of the food contrasts to the color of the plate. Do not serve food on a plate that has a busy pattern.

7. Especially if the change in diet is sudden, check his mouth for thrush (a painful yeast infection of the mouth made more likely by taking antibiotics). Look for a white film inside the mouth that cannot be scraped off. Also, watch for dental issues or jaw problems.

8. If your loved one is in a facility, make certain he is not placed at the dinner table with someone who is stealing his food.

9. Some medications may increase appetite (such as some antidepressants). Discuss these options with your loved one's physician.

10. Swallowing problems develop as a normal part of the progression of Alzheimer's disease.

11. Your loved one may "forget how to eat" and be at risk of aspiration (where food, liquids or saliva go down the windpipe).

12. Address issues of end-of-life nourishment early in the disease process before they occur.

13. Consider speech therapy to assist with swallowing problems if your loved one can still follow directions.

EATING TOO MUCH

1. Do not serve food "family style" around the table.

2. Serve your loved one's plate instead of allowing her to serve herself.

3. Do not keep junk food / candy where she can find it.

4. If she must have snacks, serve fruit, raw vegetables, and other healthy foods that are high in nutrition and low in calories.

5. If your loved one is in a facility and eats at a table with others, make certain she is placed at a table with people who know and can verbalize if she steals their food.

6. Eating too much, yet undernourished: check with her physician or a registered dietician about adding nutritional supplements like Boost or Ensure.

7. Some medications used to treat behavioral symptoms in Alzheimer's disease may cause increased appetite (antidepressants, antipsychotics, etc.). Be aware of this, and report any significant weight gain to the physician caring for your loved one.

FALSE ACCUSATIONS
(especially accusations of theft)

1. Do not argue. Your loved one's belief is very real to her.

2. Those with Alzheimer's disease often think someone is stealing from them, hiding their things, someone is out to get them, etc.

3. An inability to find things goes hand in glove with Alzheimer's disease. The person forgets where she put something; therefore, someone must have stolen it.

4. If your loved one is in a facility, someone may very well have taken whatever your loved one is looking for. Residents cannot remember what is theirs and what belongs to someone else. Label everything in permanent marker and usually, it will come back to you.

5. "Let me help you look for it," is always a good response to an accusation of theft, or "Maybe the thief dropped it around here somewhere." Begin by looking for the item, but help the person get distracted along the way. "Find" something else (old photo album, favorite CD, anything that could take the person's mind off the "stolen" item.

6. Tell your loved one whatever is necessary to allay her fears. Your mother believes her favorite bracelet has been stolen? "Mama, I took it out to be cleaned." Your husband believes someone has taken his blue sport coat? "Dear, there was a seam that had torn, so I took it home to repair it."

HALLUCINATIONS/ALTERED PERCEPTIONS

1. People with Alzheimer's disease have altered perceptions of the world that often bear little or no resemblance to reality. Hallucinations (what the person sees has no basis in reality) also are very common.

2. Reflections in mirrors, glass, etc. may look like someone else to your loved one. The person in her reflection may be friend or foe. Cover mirrors if this becomes a problem.

3. Your loved one may believe things occurring on the television or a movie screen are happening in the room with him. Monitor what he watches if this is an issue.

4. It is completely normal for those with Alzheimer's disease not to recognize people they have known all their lives or to believe a person is someone else.

5. Those with Alzheimer's disease may not remember the past or may remember it as something completely false. They often remember the distant past, but not the recent past.

6. Keep in mind always that the person's perceptions, reasoning, understanding --- everything is skewed by the disease.

7. Things that seem irrational to you are very real to your loved one. Trying to convince him otherwise (instead of soothing fears, agreeing with harmless hallucinations, or distracting / redirecting him) will only cause upset, confusion, or agitation in your loved one and may cause a violent outburst.

8. Always report new onset hallucinations and altered perceptions to your loved one's physician.

INAPPROPRIATE PUBLIC BEHAVIOR

1. Public toileting, sexual behavior, anger management issues, "hitting" on members of the opposite sex, saying inappropriate things, etc., are all relatively common issues in those with Alzheimer's disease.

2. This stage of the disease may last several months or several years, or your loved one may never exhibit these problems.

3. Stay calm. Getting angry, blaming your loved one, yelling, or similar reactions will only make things worse.

4. Try to distract the person from the behavior. It may take several tries.

5. Try to find a "hot button" issue that usually distracts the person. For some it's, "Your hair is messed up! You need to go comb it." For others it may be, "Let's go get a milkshake." Find your loved one's "hot button" issue and use it liberally.

6. For those who try to undress in public or exhibit public sexual behavior, consider a "busy apron" or "Alzheimer's apron" which has buttons, zippers, snaps, etc. all over the front, but is just about impossible for them to remove. It covers their real clothing, and keeps them from removing it. Several companies offer these over the internet.

7. Have business cards printed saying, "My husband has Alzheimer's disease. Please excuse his behavior," or something similar. Most people will be quite understanding when they know why the person is acting strangely.

8. Consider Alzheimer's disease daycare, so you as the caregiver do not become socially isolated.

9. Talk to your loved one's physician, who may recommend medication.

"I WANT TO GO HOME."

1. As Alzheimer's disease progresses, nothing looks familiar; nowhere is home. The search for home is really a search for familiarity and comfort.

2. Look at old photographs, tell old stories, listen to favorite music, read familiar texts, etc.

3. Art and music therapies, drama, dance, and storytelling can help your loved one connect to the past, and give you a way to connect with him.

4. Whatever helps the person feel safe and loved will help him feel at home.

5. Try to distract him from the subject of home.

6. Tell him you'll take him home in a little while when you finish what you are doing. Do not say to him, "You *are* at home." This is invalidating to him and could start an argument.

PERSONAL PRIVACY ISSUES

1. Often "privacy" issues cause the most upset, agitation, and violence in those with Alzheimer's disease.

2. Even those well into the mid or late stages of the disease process still may retain a great sense of modesty. Respect this.

3. When bathing her, leave her robe on until the last possible minute.

4. When dressing her, take one piece of clothing off and replace it with another (replacing one blouse with another, for instance), instead of completely disrobing her and then beginning the dressing process.

5. When giving very private care, talk about pleasant things the person may remember from the past, play the person's favorite music, or play a favorite DVD.

6. When bathing your loved one, give him a warm washcloth to hold.

7. Cover the mirrors or take them down.

8. Plan your loved one's bath at the best time of day for him, making sure that he is not hungry at the time.

9. Your loved one may not need a bath every day or even every other day. Two or three times a week may be sufficient, unless he is incontinent.

10. If your loved one is becoming violent or agitated, postpone whatever it is that is upsetting her until later, if possible. You may need to talk to her physician about medication.

REPEATED PHRASES AND STORIES

1. This is extremely common in those with Alzheimer's disease and very annoying for caregivers.

2. It probably cannot be changed.

3. Ask your loved one questions about the phrase or story, and you may be able to temporarily distract him.

SLEEPLESSNESS

1. Minimize caffeinated beverages and chocolate. Serve none whatsoever after mid-afternoon. Never give your loved one an "energy" drink.

2. Substitute de-caffeinated beverages.

3. Do not feed the person high sugar foods (desserts, candy, non-diet soft drinks, etc.) in the evening.

4. Try not to allow the person to sleep during the day.

5. Keep the person physically and mentally active.

6. Given before bedtime, warm milk with a little real vanilla extract added may make the person drowsy.

7. While sleeping, does he move frequently or snore loudly? If so, he may have Restless Legs Syndrome or sleep apnea, either of which can keep him from going into a deep sleep and can awaken him numerous times during the night. Talk to your doctor about a sleep study.

8. If these suggestions do not work, or do not work well enough, talk to your doctor about an over-the-counter or prescription sleep medication.

VIOLENCE

1. Verbal or physical abuse of the caregiver is relatively common in those with Alzheimer's disease, especially those whose frontal lobe (judgment area of the brain) is more involved.

2. It is most problematic in those who retain strength and physical ability into the later stages of the disease.

3. Things to avoid violence:

   a. If something you are doing is agitating or upsetting your loved one, stop it immediately. If it is an emergency situation, get help.

   b. Know your loved one's physical signs of agitation: increased breathing, franticness, pacing, wringing of hands, etc. When you see your loved one exhibiting these signs, stop whatever you are doing or think of another approach.

   c. Do not argue with your loved one. Agree with what she says if you can or make a neutral statement. Redirect her. Smile at her. LOVE her. Gently pat her hand or hug her if this would not be dangerous.

   d. Alcoholic beverages

4. Feed your loved one more frequent, smaller meals (or healthy snacks between meals) to help her blood sugar stay at a consistent level, giving more protein and less carbohydrates / sweets.

5. If you must do something that you know will be upsetting (bathing, doctor's appointment, etc.), choose the best time of day for your loved one.

6. Play your loved one's favorite music, talk about things you know he enjoyed in years past ("Remember the time when we were first married and we went....")

7. Remove dangerous objects (especially firearms) and substances from your loved one's environment.

8. Talk with your loved one's physician about her tendency toward physical aggression or violence. Sometimes, medication is necessary.

9. If you are in physical danger, remove yourself from the situation and call the police.

10. In the worst cases, a person with Alzheimer's disease who is violent may have to be committed through the court system. Talk to his physician and an elder law attorney if you feel your loved one may have anger management issues to this degree.

WALKING AND BALANCE PROBLEMS

1. As Alzheimer's disease progresses, it affects walking ability and balance. Your loved one will be more likely to fall.

2. Clear the floors in your home of clutter, throw rugs, spills, etc.

3. Restrict your loved one's access to stairs. If stairs must be used, install sturdy rails and only allow access when caregivers are there to help.

4. Falls often occur in the bathroom, so be sure to keep the floor dry and install rails for the tub, seats and rubber mats for the shower.

5. Do not allow your loved one to walk in sock feet, but use shoes with gripping soles and good support.

6. Avoid letting your loved one walk on uneven ground.

7. Consider canes, walkers and wheelchairs as needed. Avoid "scooters" or motorized wheelchairs unless absolutely necessary.

8. Consider the use of gait and balance training from an experienced physical therapist if your loved can still follow directions.

9. Call 911 if a fall should occur. Do not try to lift your loved one yourself.

WANDERING

1. This is one of the most potentially dangerous parts of the disease and one of the most terrifying for the caregiver.

2. If your loved one with Alzheimer's disease can walk, take precautions against wandering, even if she lives in a facility. It may save her life.

3. Investigate whether Project Lifesaver International (www.projectlifesaver.org) is available in your area. They provide GPS bracelets to anyone at risk of wandering. If Project Lifesaver is not available, check with your local senior citizen's organization to see what services are available in your area.

4. Ways to prevent wandering before it happens:

    a. Use door knob covers and keyed deadbolt locks (keeping the key around your neck for fire safety). NEVER leave a person with Alzheimer's disease unattended in a locked building.

    b. Paint doorways and doorknobs leading outside the same colors as the walls to camouflage them. Continue wallpaper borders across the doors.

    c. Place large, red "STOP" signs over doors you don't wish the person to use.

    d. Place large, black floor mats in front of doorways you don't wish the person to use. They often think it's a hole.

e. Avoid taking the person places where you will be distracted --- grocery shopping, the mall, etc. --- thereby increasing the likelihood the person could wander away

f. Take the car keys away and hide them.

Life in the Present

by Daniel C. Potts, M.D.

"Now"...

which only death can steal;

where dream meets life
and life meets memory;

where there are no expectations
or regrets...

where passing units of time infinitesimal
bring the world afresh:
innocent,
wonderful,
unknown...

where "self" is ever redefined
in context;

where God and we may co-create;

where, though briefly,
birth and death embrace
at love's behest;

where to exist is to begin
and to begin is to hope
and to hope is to live;

Let me only and always
play on your stage,
and in each singing, dancing, praying, praising line
take my cues

from Love alone.

RESOURCES

Alabama Dementia Education Training Program
www.alzbrain.org

Alzheimer's Association www.alz.org

Alzheimer's Foundation of America www.alzfdn.org

Borrie, Cathie. The Long Hello
www.cathieborrie.com

Cognitive Dynamics Foundation
www.cognitivedynamics.org

Coste, Joanne Koenig. Learning to Speak Alzheimer's,
www.learningtospeakalzheimers.com

Dementia Dynamics, LLC www.dementiadynamics.com

Fazio, Sam. The Enduring Self in People with Alzheimer's and Rethinking Alzheimer's Care

Hearthstone Alzheimer's Care www.thehearth.org

Mace, Nancy and Rabins, Peter. The 36-Hour Day: A Family Guide to Caring for People with Alzheimer's Disease, Other Dementias and Memory Loss in Later Life

Project Lifesaver International www.projectlifesaver.org

Validation Therapy Insitutute (Naomi Feil)
www.vfvalidation.org